WILLIAM ADAM 1689–174

WILLIAM ADAM
1689–1748

A Life and Times of Scotland's Universal Architect

John Gifford

MAINSTREAM
PUBLISHING

SCOTTISH EQUITABLE
SCOTTISH EQUITABLE LIFE ASSURANCE SOCIETY

The publisher gratefully acknowledges financial assistance from the Scottish Arts Council in the publication of this volume.

The production of this book has been supported by The Russell Trust, and is printed on Tricote Velvet 135 g/m^2 from Tullis Russell, The Papermakers, Markinch, Fife.

Publication of this book was made possible by the support of Historic Buildings and Monuments Directorate.

First published in Great Britain in 1989 by
MAINSTREAM PUBLISHING COMPANY (EDINBURGH) LTD
7 Albany Street
Edinburgh EH1 3UG

In conjunction with the
ROYAL INCORPORATION OF ARCHITECTS IN SCOTLAND
15 Rutland Square
Edinburgh EH1 2BE

ISBN 1 85158 295 9 (cloth)
ISBN 1 85158 296 7 (paper)

British Library Cataloguing in Publication Data

Gifford, John
    William Adam 1689–1748: a life and times of
    Scotland's universal architect
    1. Scotland. Architectural design. Adam, William,
    1689–1748
    I. Title
    720.92'41
    ISBN 1-85158-295-9
    ISBN 1-85158-296-7 pbk

Typeset in 12pt Caslon by Blackpool Typesetting Services Ltd., Blackpool
Printed in Great Britain by Butler and Tanner Ltd., Frome, Somerset.

Acknowledgements

This book came into existence largely through the activities of two gadflies of the architectural world. Charles McKean, Secretary of the Royal Incorporation of Architects in Scotland, suggested that I write it and cajoled the publishers into undertaking its production. Beginning some years before, Charles E. Peterson (perhaps more properly a horsefly) in pursuit of his researches on the Scottish-born Philadelphia architect, Robert Smith, made himself such a nuisance with his questions about early 18th-century Scotland and William Adam that I was infuriated into trying to find some of the answers.

The typescript was read by Keith Adam of Blair Adam, Catherine Cruft, Ian Gow, William Kay whose own thesis on William Adam is eagerly awaited, Colin McWilliam, and James Simpson from whose work on Adam I have drawn much. I am grateful for their comments, half-apologetic for having ignored some of them, and responsible for the remaining mistakes. Dr Iain Gordon Brown kindly allowed me to read his unpublished thesis on Sir John Clerk of Penicuik, and Dr Tristram Clarke drew my attention to the incident involving William Adam and William Duguid. The staff of the Scottish Record Office, the National Library of Scotland, the Edinburgh Central Public Library, Kirkcaldy Museum and Art Gallery, and Kirkcaldy Public Library have been unfailingly helpful. Dr Walter Makey, the then archivist, showed his habitual courtesy when I examined the records of the Incorporation of Mary's Chapel in the care of the City of Edinburgh District Council. Susannah Kerr of the Scottish National Portrait Gallery remained calm as I tried to decide on what portraits to illustrate. My biggest debt is to the staff of the National Monuments Record of Scotland, in particular Shona McGaw, whose familiarity with my working methods has not yet bred open contempt.

Claire Watts and Anna Fenge of Mainstream have proved admirable midwives for the book's appearance which could not, however, have occurred without the tenacity of Emma Crawford, of Simpson & Brown, in nosing out the sponsors whose contributions in cash and kind were required for its birth.

I am grateful to Sir John Clerk of Penicuik for permission to quote from papers deposited in the Scottish Record Office.

Keith Adam of Blair Adam: frontispiece, pp. 66, 175, 177, 182
The Duke of Buccleuch and Queensberry: p.159
Sir John Clerk of Penicuik: pp. 80, 185
Country Life: pp. 96, 97, 104, 105, 139, 140
Mr and Mrs A. Dundas-Bekker, Arniston House: p. 102
Ian Fisher: p. 146
Glasgow University: p. 166
The Earl of Haddington: p. 98
The Duke of Hamilton and Brandon: p. 64
Historic Buildings and Monuments Directorate: pp. 152, 154
Hopetoun House Preservation Trust: p. 87
Colin McWilliam: p. 56
The Earl of Mar and Kellie: p. 65
National Gallery of Scotland: p. 48
National Trust for Scotland: p. 128
Joe Rock: pp. 131, 132
Royal Commission on the Ancient and Historical Monuments of Scotland: pp. 12, 19, 42, 50, 53, 54, 55, 58, 59, 60, 85, 88, 89, 91, 95, 100, 101, 103, 113, 114, 115, 116, 117, 118, 119, 120, 121, 123, 125, 126, 130, 132, 135, 144, 145, 146, 149, 153, 158, 161, 164, 165, 167, 168, 169, 170, 173, 174
The Royal Incorporation of Architects in Scotland: 148, 172
Scottish National Portrait Gallery: 52, 78, 134, 143, 184

Contents

William Adam

INTRODUCTION

For contemporaries in early eighteenth-century Scotland William Adam's position as 'the universal architect' of that country was unquestioned. In Scotland today his surviving buildings are treasured. House of Dun and Haddo House are owned by the National Trust for Scotland; Duff House is in the care of the Secretary of State; Chatelherault, after its purchase by the National Land Fund and restoration under the supervision of the Historic Buildings and Monuments Directorate, is now the pride of Hamilton District Council, and Mavisbank will now survive after a long struggle by private individuals, conservationist groups and local and central government.

By our contemporaries outside Scotland he is honoured as the father of Robert and James Adam while a few know him as the author of *Vitruvius Scoticus*, some of whose engravings have been claimed as the sources for designs of houses in Ireland and America built before that book's publication. But they have been too ready to see him as a provincial follower of English architects without placing him in the context of the Scotland of his day which was still, in its economic life, its social assumptions and its way of thinking, almost a foreign country.

It is as the architect of Scotland that William Adam must be understood and celebrated.

Chapter 1

THE SCOTTISH BACKGROUND

The Scotland into which William Adam was born in 1689 and where he died in 1748 was a semi-feudal country only beginning to be touched by ideas of economic and social advance. Much of the heavier and potentially most fertile land was then undrained marsh. Most of the lowlands and north-east was almost bare of trees while parts of the Highlands were covered with forest. The few roads were often impassable by wheeled traffic.

It was an overwhelmingly rural society. Probably more than nine tenths of its population of about one million lived on and from that quarter of the surface area which was fit for any sort of cultivation.[1] Here they practised subsistence agriculture of a type known as runrig which, despite regional variations, was general throughout Scotland. Each farm, generally of less than 100 acres,[2] was jointly tenanted by groups of between four and sixteen families who lived, together with farm labourers and rural craftsmen, in a hamlet (the ferm-toun) at the centre of the arable land.[3] From the hamlet stretched fields unbroken by dykes or hedges to rough pasture, moor or marsh. The arable land formed two concentric rings, the inner being the infield, the outer the outfield. The infield was broken up into 200–500 yard long S-shaped ridged strips (rigs) whose curvy outline was probably caused by the difficulty of driving in a straight line the team of six to ten horses or oxen which pulled the heavy but inefficient Scots plough. Between the rigs lay hollows or 'baulks' of uncultivated ground covered with rough pasture and weeds. All the infield's rigs were cultivated each year, following a rudimentary rotation of crops (often one crop of the coarse Scots barley, known as bere, followed by two of oats). After harvest the farm livestock was allowed to graze on the stubble, contributing some manure to the land in return. In the spring the rigs about to be sown with bere were manured with the dung, which had been produced during the winter by the beasts housed in stables or byres, to which was added the peat-smoke impregnated thatch stripped from the roofs of the tenants' houses.[4]

View of Brechin from John Slezer, Theatrum Scotiae

The outfield, also divided into strips, had as its main purpose the growing of oats. Since the only manure it usually received came from the controlled pasturing of beasts during spring and summer, only about one third of it was cultivated at a time, the remainder lying fallow for several years after cultivation until natural recuperation again allowed it to produce a crop.[5] In some parts of Scotland more intensive cultivation of outfield land and perhaps its enlargement was made possible, from the early seventeenth century, by the spreading of lime on the ground,[6] a practice deplored by the physician Sir Robert Sibbald in 1698 as fatal to fish and injurious to human health but which was largely responsible for the fact he also noted, that 'ther is a vast deal of Ground now tilled and Laboured which befor was in pastur.'[7]

The pasture of the uncultivated parts of the outfield was supplemented by grazing on the moor, hill or waste land beyond. In some areas such as Ayrshire and Galloway this could support sizeable numbers of cattle,[8] but lack of drainage too often meant that this pasture consisted of little more than sedge-grass and rushes.[9]

Winter feed for livestock was in short supply. Hay was not normally grown as a crop before the end of the eighteenth century although some bog-hay might be made from the grass and rushes growing beyond the outfield.[10] Root crops such as turnips were not used for animal fodder before the mid-eighteenth century.[11] Consequently there was a large slaughter of cattle each Martinmas, the carcasses being salted down for food,[12] and the hides providing one of the country's principal exports.[13] Many other beasts were sold to England for fattening on sheltered southern pastures.[14] Those exempted from slaughter or export were wintered in byres but so poorly fed that they sometimes had to be carried to the pasture in spring.[15]

The quality of livestock and crops was poor. Scottish sheep, of which most farms had a few,[16] and cattle (known by the English as 'Scotch runts') were notoriously small, although Sibbald proclaimed their meat to be 'of ane fine taste and very nourishing'.[17] Peas and beans were grown in some areas, as was wheat in the Lothians and rye in the Hebrides. In the south-east a little hemp was grown for home-made harness, ropes and bags. Most places produced some flax for making into linen.[18] But the principal crops were bere and bristle-pointed oats, which were capable of growing on acidic soil and were wind resistant. However, they gave a low yield – a three-fold return on seed being considered generally satisfactory and a four-fold one good.[19] Such returns meant that between a quarter and a third of the produce had to be retained for seed.[20]

Rents for arable land were largely paid in kind,[21] about one third of the average crop going to the landlord.[22] In addition the landlord received the tiend (the tithe or tenth sheaf), a stipulated amount of poultry and dairy produce and miscellaneous items like woollen yarn and straw ropes. The tenant's obligations to his laird were not limited to the payment of rent. He had to provide labour at seedtime and harvest and carriage service for the transport of agricultural produce and building materials. Usually he was bound to the laird's mill to which he had to take his grain, pay a proportion of his produce, and for whose maintenance and repair he had to provide labour service. The tenant's final indignity was to suffer the sight of the landowner's pigeons, a staple source of winter food for the gentry, emerging from their doocots to stuff themselves on his crops.[23]

The organisation of this agricultural system was governed by law. The annual redistribution of rigs among joint tenants and the settlement of their minor differences was made by the birley court composed of the tenants under one of their number.[24] On each estate there was also a Baron Court, usually presided over by the laird's factor, with civil and criminal jurisdiction over

most matters including differences between landlord and
tenant.[25] There was truth as well as some exaggeration in the
Englishman Thomas Kirke's diatribe against Scottish society in
1679:

> The nobility and gentry Lord it over their poor tenants, and use
> them worse than galley-slaves; they are all bound to serve them,
> men, women, and children; the first fruits is always the landlord's
> due . . . Every laird (of note) hath a gibet near his house, and has
> power to condemne and hang any one of his vassals . . .[26]

Powerful the laird might be in respect to his tenants but their
labour did not necessarily make him rich. In Angus in 1683 the
income from rents on estates varied from £31 Scots to £2,300
Scots (£2 10s. 2d. to £100 18s. 4d. sterling), in Banffshire in 1690
from £20 Scots to £1,200 Scots.[27] In 1723 William Mackintosh of
Borlum estimated that an estate had usually to contain 400–800
acres of arable and meadow land to provide a rental of £1,200
Scots (£100 sterling) and that 'a great many' estates 'possest by
Gentlemen of very good Families' were worth only £240–£1,200
Scots (£20–£100 sterling) per annum.[28] Besides his income from
the tenants' rents the laird usually cultivated a mains, or home
farm, employing farm servants whose maximum wages were
fixed annually by the Justices of the Peace.[29] But the mains farm
was not always a model. Andrew Fletcher of Saltoun thought that:

> . . . the unskilfulness of their wretched and half-starved servants
> is such, that their lands are no better cultivated than those
> laboured by beggarly tenants. And though a gentleman of estate
> take a farm into his own hands, yet servants are so unfaithful or
> lazy, and the country people such enemies of all manner of
> inclosure, that after having struggled with innumerable dif-
> ficulties, he at last finds it impossible for him to alter the ordinary
> bad methods, whilst the rest of the country continues in them.[30]

Through the seventeenth and early eighteenth centuries this
unimproved Scottish agriculture was generally successful in supporting the population,[31] although with a normal number of
vagrants estimated by writers in 1698 as of the order of 100,000
or one in ten.[32] Years of bad harvest brought destitution as happened in the 1690s when Sibbald reported that 'every day whole
families abandon their houses and Beg, not only idle and infirme

people but even Tenents & tradesmen who lived well befor',[33] the number of vagrants doubled,[34] and the population of many parishes fell by as much as a half.[35]

The backwardness of Scottish agriculture was recognised by the Scottish Parliament's successive Acts passed between 1661 and 1695 designed to encourage enclosure,[36] the preamble to the last speaking of:

> . . . the great Disadvantage arising to the whole Subjects from Lands lying run-rig, and that the same is highly prejudicial to the Policy and Improvement of the Nation, by planting and inclosing . . .[37]

In 1697 the Edinburgh journalist James Donaldson published *Husbandry Anatomized* in which he advocated better use of manure, the hedging and enclosure of fields and farms, and fallowing, and warned against overstocking with cattle. Two years later Lord Belhaven gave similar advice to East Lothian farmers in *The Country-Man's Rudiments*. In 1723 a group of nobles and lairds formed a Society for Improving the Knowledge of Agriculture which published in 1724 a *Treatise concerning the Manner of Fallowing the Ground*, and in 1729 William Mackintosh of Borlum produced *An Essay on Ways and Means for Inclosing, Fallowing, Planting, &c. Scotland.*[38] This theory of improved agriculture was put sporadically into practice. Fallowing was introduced on the East Lothian farm of Beanston about 1690 and taken up by the sixth Earl of Haddington, a noted encloser and planter of trees. One of the best known of the early eighteenth-century East Lothian improvers was John Cockburn of Ormiston who abolished runrig on his estate which he divided into single-tenant farms, each with its steading, enclosures and plantations. He also founded a local agricultural society which met for monthly discussions.[39] In the fertile area around the Moray Firth English ploughs and ploughmen were introduced by Lady Elizabeth Mordaunt soon after her marriage to the Marquess of Huntly in 1706,[40] and extensive drainage operations carried out by Sir Robert Gordon of Gordonstoun and Sir William Gordon of Invergordon.[41] Still further north Lieutenant-General Charles Ross, who acquired the Balnagown estate in 1713, 'did not only fallow his Mains himself, but impos'd Fallowing on his Tenants . . .'[42] From about 1720 Galloway landowners such as Gordon of Earlstoun and Lady Kenmure developed their estates for cattle,

amalgamating small farms into large units, enclosing and expand-
ing pasture ground at the expense of arable, and finding a
memorial in the ballad which expressed the feelings of their
dispossessed tenantry:

> Against the poor the lairds prevail
> With all their wicked works,
> Who will enclose both hill and dale,
> And turn cornfields to parks.[43]

But these improvements, real enough though they were and significant forerunners of the changes which were to revolutionise
Scottish agriculture after 1750, were relatively few and far
between. When William Adam set himself up as the laird of Blair-
Crambeth in 1731 he took over an estate quite unimproved,
entirely lacking enclosures or plantations.[44]

What lay under the land could be as important for some lairds
as the crops it could grow. Coal mining had been practised in
Scotland since the Middle Ages but expanded significantly in the
seventeenth century,[45] the quality of the product being praised
by Thomas Morer in 1689 ('so bituminous and pitchy that it burns
like a candle, and is both pleasant and useful').[46] The main field
lay along the Firth of Forth where at the end of the sixteenth
century Sir George Bruce of Carnock had exploited the coal
seams at Culross.[47] The developing industry was served by new
harbours like those built by the Earl of Winton at Port Seton, the
Earl of Wemyss at Methil, and, for the Ayrshire coalfield, by Sir
Robert Cunningham of Auchenharvie at Saltcoats.[48]

Often associated with the mines were salt pans, the coal providing the fuel needed to boil sea water, and miners and salters
were linked in a series of seventeenth-century Acts of Parliament.
The first, passed in 1606, provided that a collier or salter who
deserted his employment was to be deemed a thief for having
stolen himself from his master and gave 'power and commission
to all masters and owners of coal-heughs and salt pans to
apprehend all vagabonds and sturdy beggars to be put to labour.'
By the late seventeenth century miners and salters generally
either bound themselves to their employment for a year and a
day or, by taking 'arles' or earnest money, bound themselves for
life. It was common for miners to arle their children at their
baptism.[49] Semi-slave labour did not, however, solve the peren-
nial problem of flooding of the coal seams. At Culross Sir George

Bruce had channelled a burn to drive a waterwheel which worked a chain of buckets raising water from the workings. Later, he used a horse-powered wheel.[50] In 1620 Samuel Johnstone of Elphinstone received a patent for a new method of draining pits,[51] and in 1701 the architect James Smith obtained another for a version of the English Savery steam pump which he had altered 'to considerable advantage so that in the short space of an hour there may be raised thereby no less than the quantity of twenty tuns of water to the hight of fourteen fathoms . . .'[52] Primitive steam pumps were installed at Stevenston in Ayrshire in 1719 and Elphinstone in Stirlingshire about 1720 but these were of use only in shallow pits and it was not until after 1750 that efficient pumps were widely used.[53] Even though much of the coal was probably burnt in Scotland (mainly by the gentry and in the burghs, according to Morer)[54] the recorded annual exports of less than 20,000 tons (worth about £67,000 Scots or about £5,500 sterling) suggest that the industry was primarily of local importance.[55] Of even less significance among Scottish exports but important for its building industry was the lead extracted from the Earl of Hopetoun's mine at Leadhills and the Duke of Queensberry's at Wanlockhead.[56]

Scotland's rivers and seas housed fish which made up a major source of food for her population and, in the form of salmon and salted herring, an export commodity. Netting on the Don, the Dee, the Forth, the Tay and the Tweed provided most of the salmon of which exports worth £200,000 Scots were sent to France and Holland in 1669. The herring fishery was conducted mostly inshore by small boats which unloaded their catches at the east coast ports of Dunbar, Crail and Anstruther, and the west coast port of Greenock where they were salted and packed before sale to Edinburgh and Glasgow merchants for sale abroad. Unsuccessful attempts were made, notably by the Royal Fishing Company founded in 1670 and wound up twenty years later 'all turned to loss and disappointment', to set up a herring fishery on Dutch lines by which a large catching fleet of small boats serviced mother-ships or 'busses' on which the catch was packed and salted and taken direct to market.[57] That aristocrats could be involved in fishing as well as mining is shown by the Earl of Errol's application of 1684 to the Privy Council, for help in securing the return of two fishermen who had left his employment. He stated that 'the seamen of fish boats in the North Country are by the constant custom of the place tyed and obleidged to the same servitud and service that coall hewars and salters are here in the South.'[58]

Manufacturing industry was small-scale, dominated by the making of linens and woollen cloth. Despite the success of a Leith factory making woollen stockings, its example followed by establishments in Aberdeenshire and Ayrshire, the woollen industry was already in decline by the late seventeenth century,[59] and virtually collapsed after 1707 when the Act of Union exposed Scotland to the perils and delights of free trade with England.[60] The linen industry had grown during the seventeenth century so that by its end it was exporting annually between 1,200,000 and 1,800,000 ells of 'Scotch linen' worth £400,000–£650,000 Scots.[61] The immediate effect of the Act of Union's opening of the Scottish market to Irish and Continental linens was the collapse of Scotland's small fine linen industry without any marked growth in her export of coarse linen.[62] However, in 1727 the Government set up a Board of Trustees for Manufactures to spend money which had been allocated by the Act of Union to stimulate the trade in coarse wool. The Trustees immediately allocated £2,650 to the linen industry, offering premiums for the growth of better quality flax and the introduction of new methods of scutching and heckling which prepared the flax for spinning.[63] In 1729 they sent James Spalding of Bonnington Mills near Edinburgh to Holland to study scutching techniques. On his return the next year he built a water-powered scutching mill, the first of several erected in the 1730s.[64] At the same time there were set up several large-scale bleachfields with full-time professional staff.[65] The Bounty Act of 1742 which granted subsidies for exports of British linen boosted the trade between the Clyde and the American colonies where rough cloth was much in demand. In 1746 the British Linen Company was established to promote the export of Scottish linen especially to America and Africa although it soon turned its energies to banking by extending credit to manufacturers.[66] The success of the Board of Manufactures is shown by the increase in production of Scottish linen for sale from an annual average of 3.5 million yards (worth an estimated £132,600 sterling) in 1728–32 to 7.2 million yards (worth £350,800) twenty years later.[67] But even with these developments, linen-making was still very largely a rural cottage industry.[68] Much less important, although some were to become of significance in the late eighteenth century, were the many new industries founded between the Restoration and the Act of Union. In the rapidly

developing burgh of Glasgow alone the years between 1667 and 1707 saw the establishment of soap making, sugar refining and rum distilling, rope making, hardware, glass, porcelain and earthenware factories as well as a paper mill. Some of these survived the increased English competition after the Act of Union.[69]

View of Perth from John Slezer, Theatrum Scotiae

Most of the nation's commerce was conducted in the burghs. By 1707 there were sixty-six royal burghs,[70] and one hundred and ninety-one burghs of barony.[71] The burghs of barony of which more than half had been created since the Restoration were often no more than villages and almost always under the control of the local landowner for whose benefit they had been created.[72] Primarily they were local trading centres and homes for craftsmen. Colinsburgh in Fife was typical of the smaller burghs of barony. A village here was laid out in the 1680s and named after the landowner Colin, Earl of Balcarres. In 1707 the Earl obtained a Crown charter erecting a burgh of barony with the right to hold a weekly market on Tuesdays 'for buying and selling all goods, merchant-ware and merchandise whatsoever' and to have two eight-day fairs each year, one in June, the other in October. The burgh council's bailies were to be appointed by the Earl who also had the right to hold a court in the burgh.[73] Some burghs of barony were much larger, like the Duchess of Buccleuch's burgh of Dalkeith near Edinburgh, or the Duchess of Hamilton's burgh

of Bo'ness which grew rapidly in the post-Restoration period as
the Forth port serving Glasgow's trade with the east coast and
Europe.[74]

Royal burghs had traditionally been of much greater importance. In terms of the prevailing feudal system of land tenure their
corporations of burgesses held the burgh land directly from the
Crown which had granted them extensive trading rights and
privileges, to which they paid tax, and in whose parliaments they
were represented. Throughout the medieval period the conduct
of Scotland's foreign trade was almost entirely restricted to the
merchant burgesses of the royal burghs. These privileges were
confirmed by Parliament in 1661 but in 1672 the royal burghs'
monopoly of foreign trade was limited to imports of wine, wax,
silks, spices and dye-stuffs. The old extensive monopoly was
theoretically restored in 1690 but this was followed by an agreement allowing the burghs of barony a full share in foreign trade in
return for a contribution of ten per cent of the burghs' taxation.[75]

Any burgh, whether royal or baronial, restricted the right to
work at a craft within its bounds to its own freemen organised in
guilds or incorporations to which entry was by hereditary right,
right of marriage, or by payment after serving an apprenticeship
to a freeman of the burgh. Apprentices might be drawn from out-
with the burgh. Thus, in 1748 John Cadell of Haddington nego-
tiated to apprentice his son to the Dalkeith weaver John Gray
having thought it his duty 'to find out a Master for him That not
only Could Teach his Buseness but Even be An Exambill to him
in Following the way of the God of his Freather [sic.] and to hav
him Traind up in the Good ould way of our Lord'.[76] If John Cadell
seems to have been as much concerned with his son's spiritual
welfare as his learning the weaving trade, the father of Thomas
Mitchell who was sent from Alloa in 1668 as apprentice to the
Stirling merchant Andrew Russell was clearly intent on his son's
future worldly success. Thomas Mitchell was to be instructed in
all the arts of merchandising, be sent to London, Holland and elsewhere on at least three separate occasions and be put in a Dutch
school to learn that language and arithmetic. This breadth of
education for a prospective merchant was not unique. In 1686 the
Edinburgh merchant Alexander Brand asked Russell, by then
living in Rotterdam, to enter his apprentice in a school where he
could learn Dutch, arithmetic and bookkeeping, 'and also wher
he may meet with no other Scots lads except ye know them to
be such as he may be bettered by in their Company . . .'[77]

The merchant guilds and trade incorporations which jointly governed royal burghs could be tenacious of their position in excluding outsiders from working. In 1678 after his tools had been confiscated by the Edinburgh Incorporation of Wrights, James Turner appealed to the Privy Council claiming that he had learnt the art of making cabinets, mirror glasses, dressing boxes, chests of drawers, 'comb boxes, spatch and pouder boxes, and the like curious work . . . not formerly practised by any native of this countrey, and which art or trade does noeways interfeir or encroach upon the calling of the wrights . . . priviledged in the incorporation of wrights, being a manufactor by it selfe.'[78] The wrights were ordered to stop troubling Turner but in 1685 he again appealed to the Privy Council after the Incorporation had had him fined £20 sterling for encroaching on their privileges.[79] In 1704 the Earl of Hopetoun asked for the Privy Council's authority to allow repair of his windmill at Leith by a certain John Smith whose work had been interfered with violently by the wrights of Edinburgh, 'albeit it is sufficiently known that none of these have been bred to such work or have any skill therein'.[80]

The level of craftsmen's skills was generally proportionate to the size of a burgh and most of the royal burghs were very small. In 1707, Edinburgh, by far the largest, had a population of about 40,000. Then came Glasgow with about 12,000, followed by Dundee, Aberdeen and Perth, each with about 4,000. The coastal burghs of the East Neuk of Fife had only a few hundred each.[81] The effects on the royal burghs of their loss of foreign trade in the late seventeenth century were made worse by the raising of English tariffs against Scottish goods and the loss of the hitherto important French market by the wars against France after 1688. In 1692 each royal burgh reported on its condition to the Convention of Royal Burghs. Even allowing for much self-pitying exaggeration the picture was bleak. Stirling reported foreign trade worth less than 20,000 merks a year, 'no Inland trade' and retail trade in its shops 'not exceeding 10,000 marks yearly in the haill.' Its inhabitants looked enviously at the nearby baronial burghs such as Falkirk, Alloa, Doune and Dunblane 'who have a considerable trade and are very prejudiciall to them.'[82] Linlithgow had a 'very inconsiderable' foreign trade, inland trade of only about '10,000 weight of tallow and 1600 or 1800 sheep skines' a year and complained of competition from the baronial burghs of Bo'ness, Grangepans, Kirkliston, Torphichen and Bathgate.[83] In East Lothian, Haddington reported 'some little inconsiderable

trade in Inglish goodes and Holland goodes', the export of two or
three thousand skins a year, and inland trade 'not worth the noti-
ceing, being only manadged by poor packmen'. Again the town's
decline was contrasted with the condition of nearby burghs of
barony 'which are now more frequented and more buying and
selling of goods therein then in Hadingtoun'.[84] In Dysart two-
thirds of the burgh was 'either uninhabitat or ruinous'.[85] Over the
past ten years Kirkcaldy had lost nineteen ships (seventeen by
sinking, one by sale and one to a privateer) and now had only fourteen ships engaged in foreign trade, principally shipping coal to
Holland and London, as well as four ferry boats.[86] In Angus,
Brechin had no foreign trade and its inland trade was 'very mean
and small, being altogether failed within these three or four years
last, soe that more then a third pairt of the merchants and
inhabitants of the toune are either become bankrupt or left the
burgh...'[87] Pittenweem stated that 'As to the forraigne and inland
trade, ther is non in this place...'[88] Selkirk's only trade was in
the manufacture and sale of shoes.[89] In the west, Renfrew, without
foreign trade and with inland trade 'not worth the nameying',
regarded jealously the neighbouring burghs of barony, 'all which
are in a flourishing condition'.[90] At Tain in Ross-shire, 'a great pairt
of the building of this poor place is waist and turned ruinous...'[91]
In Perth there were 'many and sewerall ruinous lands and
decayed houses'.[92] Aberdeen's Town Council had a budget deficit
of £7,000 or £8,000 Scots and was unable to get credit.[93] The
burghs' self-portrait in 1692 was not inconsistent with Thomas
Kirke's description of them thirteen years before:

> Their cities are poor and populous, especially Edenborough, their
> metropolis, which so well suits with the inhabitants that one
> character will serve them both, viz., high and dirty.[94]

The poverty of many royal burghs was both a cause and an
effect of a general lack of capital for investment. Matters were not
substantially improved by the founding of the Bank of Scotland
in 1695. For its first twenty-five years it had a subscribed capital
of only £10,000,[95] and acted as little more than a clearing house,
not taking deposits or offering cash credits.[96] Only after the for-
mation of the Royal Bank of Scotland in 1727 with a capital of
about £150,000,[97] was there a banking system of much use to the
economy. Much of the country's spare capital in the 1690s had
been invested in the Darien scheme, a completely unsuccessful

attempt to establish a Scottish colony on the isthmus of Panama as an entrepôt for the trade of the Atlantic and Pacific oceans. When the company was finally wound up by the Act of Union, almost all its capital of about £153,000 had been lost.[98] The money had been entirely raised in Scotland, almost all from individuals subscribing between £100 and £3,000. Although the formidable Anne, Duchess of Hamilton, could afford to lose her £3,000,[99] the collapse must have been serious for quite a number of the more than a hundred nobles and gentry who had each subscribed at least £1,000, twice the salary fixed for a judge of the Court of Session from 1707,[100] and five times the annual allowance settled by his father on Sir John Clerk of Penicuik when he married Lady Margaret Stewart in 1701.[101]

English visitors blamed the landowners for Scotland's lack of enterprise. In 1723 John Macky wrote:

> ... the Men here are not so usefully employ'd as in *England*: There the Production of every County is improv'd by Joint-Stocks amongst the Inhabitants of the several Counties. Iron-Works, Lead-Works, Manufactories, and every Thing else that may conduce to the common Welfare of the Nation, are set on foot, and carry'd on. But here, altho' their Rivers plentifully abound with Salmon for Exportation, their Coasts with white Fish and Herrings, more than any other in *Europe*; yet the Gentry, or Landed Men, never concern themselves about it, as a Thing below them; and leave those Improvements to Burghers of Towns, who for want of a sufficient Stock, are not able to carry on.[102]

Similarly Daniel Defoe when considering the state of Kirkcudbright in 1724 ('a Harbour without Ships, a Port without Trade, a Fishery without Nets, a People without Business')[103] put much of the blame for its poverty on the lairds:

> ... as the People have no Hands (that is, no Stock) to work, so the Gentry have no Genius to Trade; 'tis a Mechanism which they scorn; tho' their Estates are not able to feed them, they will not turn their Hands to Business or Improvement; they had rather see their Sons made Foot Soldiers, (than which as Officers treat them now there is not a more abject Thing on Earth), than see them apply to Trade, nay to Merchandize, or to the Sea, because those Things are not (forsooth) fit for Gentlemen.[104]

There were landowners who invested in industry. John
Cockburn of Ormiston, not content with the improvement of his
farms, rebuilt the village of Ormiston where he founded a
brewery, distillery and bleachfield.[105] But society was still
strongly hierarchical and conservative, even reactionary, in its
concern with status. Some of the flavour of early eighteenth-
century social attitudes can be obtained from reading Adam
Petrie's *Rules of Good Deportment* published in Edinburgh in
1720, for example from the instructions as to how to receive a
noble visitor:

> If a person of Quality makes you a Visit, and gives you notice, you
> should meet him with your Friends and best Equipage: If he sur-
> prises you, wait on him from his Coach, and conduct him to your
> best Room, and let him have the best Seat, and place your self in
> a Chair without Arms, if there be any such in the Room, and sit
> at a Distance from him; and when he removes wait upon him to
> his Coach, and see that you have your Horses in Readiness to wait
> upon him a Part of the way; and when you are to return back, take
> your leave of him courteously, acknowledging the Sense you have
> of the Honour his Lordship hath put upon you, in giving himself
> the Trouble to visit you.[106]

Petrie's assumption that the visitor would travel by coach
indicates that he was referring to a noble. Despite the paucity and
appalling condition of the roads, so that in 1680 the road between
Edinburgh and Haddington was too badly rutted to be safe for
wheeled traffic, a coach was the mark of the magnate.[107] In 1689
Thomas Morer noted that:

> . . . their great men often travel with coach and six, but with so
> much caution, that, besides their own attendance, they have a
> lusty running footman on each side the coach, to manage and
> keep it in rough places.[108]

Outside the Lowlands coaches were rare. The Duke of Atholl
seems to have owned the only one in Perthshire in 1713.[109] The
first coach to be seen at Inverness appeared in 1725 when, wrote
Edmund Burt, 'An Elephant, publicly exposed in one of the
Streets of London, could not have excited greater Admiration.'[110]
They were also expensive. In 1693 the Privy Council granted the
cabinet-maker William Scott an eleven-year monopoly 'for
making of coaches, chariots, sedans, and calashes', he having
represented that their import:

... not only occasions the yearly export of a great deal of money
out of the kingdom, but likewise that the lieges cannot be furnished
with such necessars when they have occasion for them, without
bringing them from abroad at a double charge, beside sea-hazard.[111]

Despite Scott's enterprise it was not until the 1730s, after John
Home's return to Edinburgh from serving an apprenticeship in
London, that Scottish coach-building seems to have begun in
earnest.[112] Most lairds travelled on horseback but, if of any importance, were generally accompanied by one or two running
footmen.[113]

Ownership of a coach was one expression of status. Another
was to be waited upon by liveried servants whose dress, however,
might prove more costly than their wages or board.[114] In 1679
Thomas Kirke found that:

> The nobility show themselves very great before strangers, who are
> conducted into the house by a many servants where the lord with
> his troop of shadows receives them with the grand law ... [115]

The first Earl of Seafield 'had always ten or a dozen footmen in
full liveries, fat jolly fellows, for his lordship neither liked lean
men nor lean horses.'[116] In 1698 Andrew Fletcher wrote contemp-
tuously of the typical Scottish aristocrat with 'a family in most
things composed like that of a prince, and a multitude of idle servants to consume his estate.'[117] Defoe said of the Duke of Atholl
in 1724:

> The Pomp and State in which this Noble Person Lives is not to be
> imitated in *Great Britain*; for he is served like a Prince, and main-
> tains a greater Equipage and Retinue then five Times his Estate
> would support in another Country.[118]

In legal documents the Duke was described as 'High and mighty
Prince.'[119] The same terms were applied to the Duchess of Buccleuch of whom it was related that when she dined at Dalkeith
Castle only her relatives were permitted to sit, the other guests
standing, while she was served by pages on bended knee.[120]

The status of a noble could be most powerfully, if least usefully,
expressed at his funeral. When the Duke of Lauderdale was
buried at Haddington in 1683 several years after his fall from
power, there were at least two thousand horsemen present,

'inasmuch as they filled the high way for four full miles in lenth', as well as '25 Cotches'.[121] Of exceptional grandeur was the funeral at Edinburgh in 1703 of the Duke of Rothes, Lord High Chancellor of Scotland. The procession from St Giles' to Holyrood Abbey was led by the Commander-in-Chief with two adjutant generals, the Governor of Edinburgh Castle, two regiments of soldiers and an artillery train. Reminders of mortality, a little banner painted with a skull and an hourglass, were then carried by two men followed by fifty-one poor men, each with a banner bearing the Duke's coat of arms, representing the years of his life. There then came a trumpeter preceding a knight in full armour. After gentlemen carrying heraldic banners, more gentlemen of the name of Leslie, the Duke's family name, carried his armour and two liveried lackeys led his ordinary saddle-horse in front of the main body of mourners grouped according to official or social position with the Lord Provost and Council of Edinburgh at the front, the Lords of Session and advocates in the middle, and dukes at the back. The coats of arms of the Duke's ancestors were carried by lairds, heralds bore emblems of his nobility, caparisoned horses were led by lackeys. The coffin itself was carried by fifteen noblemen and a canopy above it by twenty-one noblemen's sons and was followed by the chief family mourners. The procession ended with the Duke's coach and a troop of Guards.[122] Exceptional in its scale, this funeral was not, however, exceptional in its arrangements. The ordinary nobleman's or gentlemen's funeral procession was led by a man carrying a little banner painted with a skull, followed by as many poor men as corresponded with the deceased's age, servants bearing banners with the family's coat of arms, and eight or sixteen gentlemen carrying the arms of the dead man's ancestors.[123] It is not perhaps surprising that in 1677 the Lord Lyon King of Arms granted an Aberdeen merchant James Skene a commission:

> to marshal and condescend on the order to be observed in all funerals of Noblemen, Bishops and Gentlemen benorth the Water of Esk, the samyn order being always usual and consinant to true Heraldry.[124]

Heraldry was clearly in evidence at Sir Robert Munro of Foulis' interment in 1729 which was attended by over six hundred horsemen. According to a correspondent of the *Edinburgh Evening Courant*:

The corpse was carried on a bier betwixt two horses fully harnessed in deepest mourning. A gentleman rode in deep mourning before the corpse, uncovered, attended by two grooms and four running-footmen, all in deep mourning. The friends followed immediately behind the corpse, and the gentlemen in the rear. The scutcheons were the handsomest I ever saw . . . [125]

Presumably these escutcheons were not only handsome but also heraldically correct, unlike the one displayed in 1732 at the funeral of Colonel Francis Charteris of Amisfield whose daughter, the Countess of Wemyss, was fined by the Court of the Lord Lyon for exhibiting an unregistered coat of arms which belonged to another family.[126] Not perhaps surprisingly in view of the trouble and expense of such funerals some nobles opted for simplicity, like the first Duke of Atholl whose instructions of 1724 stated that 'I desire that my body may be buryed without any pomp', modestly requesting 'That there be not above therty or Forty noblemen, gentlemen, and Ministers invited to my funeral . . .'[127]

The state maintained by the Scottish nobility in the late seventeenth and early eighteenth centuries was a visible expression of their perhaps sentimental view of themselves as still being a feudal baronage. Mackintosh of Borlum attacked the continuance of feudal superiorities as financially harmful to the landowners and as bringing only imaginary advantage in the raising of armed men.[128] Nevertheless, in certain areas nobles were legally sub-kings, their right to heritable jurisdictions explicitly safeguarded in the Act of Union. These jurisdictions included about one hundred and sixty courts of regality, some covering very small areas like the regality of Kilwinning which comprised two parishes, others of great extent like the regality of Atholl or the Duke of Argyll's jurisdiction over 500 square miles. Within these regalities all civil and criminal cases except high treason were judged in the regality's own courts and not the royal courts.[129] A hint of the reality of that power is conveyed by a letter of 1681 from the Marquess of Atholl agreeing to lend his hangman to the burgh of Perth on condition:

yt quhen I or any of my deputs cales for him for execouting of any y^t sall be found giltie w^t in my regalities or Intrest y^t they may haue him, and he sall be returned to you Imeadlie y^{r}efter.'[130]

Strictly there was no right of appeal from the regalian courts to the royal courts although after 1707 the Court of Session began without authority to hear appeals. Besides the nobles with regalian powers landowners held many of the sheriffdoms, stewartries and bailieries of the royal courts by hereditary right; the actual judicial work was usually done by deputes.[131] After the abolition of all these heritable jurisdictions in 1747, with only the baron courts surviving with much reduced powers, the Government paid compensation of almost £165,000, the Duke of Argyll alone receiving £21,000.[132] These recompensed former owners of regalian rights may have been lucky to have received so much. The Jacobite risings of 1715 and 1745 had shown that the ability of a laird to produce a sizeable body of armed tenants was not dependent on his having regalian jurisdiction. Fear of being turned out of a farm or genuine loyalty to a laird or a chief might be as important to the tenant as any more formally legal subordination.

Scotland's central administration between the restoration of the monarchy in 1660 and the Act of Union of 1707, was controlled by the officers of state, the chief being the Lord High Chancellor, and the Scottish Privy Council composed very largely of nobles. The Scottish Parliament was less of a rubber-stamp than it had been in the early seventeenth century but had little impact on daily government. The Act of Union followed in 1708 by the abolition of the Scottish Privy Council produced a significant alteration in the workings of government. Legislative and ultimate political power moved to Westminster, as did the sixteen representative peers and forty-six members of the Parliament of Great Britain. The administrative functions of the Scottish Privy Council were largely taken over by the new Court of Exchequer and Boards of Customs, Excise and Police, all based in Edinburgh. To control the Scottish representatives in Parliament the Government chose a 'Scottish minister' who acted both as political manager and lobbyist for Scottish interests, the role filled from 1725 to 1761 by the Earl of Ilay who succeeded his brother as third Duke of Argyll in 1743. But the 'Scottish minister' was necessarily resident in London and had to entrust the day to day management of Scottish affairs to an unofficial sub-minister in Edinburgh. Under Ilay that position was filled by the judge Andrew Fletcher, Lord Milton, who manipulated elections and disposed of the hundreds of Government posts with great efficiency.[133] But it would be wrong to see Lord Milton as solely a political manager. His political involvement was part, albeit an important part, of his place as Ilay's 'man of affairs' in Edinburgh, the manager of his patron's financial and legal interests in Scotland. As such Lord Milton was one among many Edinburgh lawyers and judges, almost all from landed families and themselves the owners of estates, who managed the affairs of Scotland's nobility and lairds, sat on Government boards and commissions, and ensured the smooth running of politics and administration. It was among these lawyers and their patrons that William Adam found his clients.

Chapter 2

THE BUILDING TRADE

For the huge majority of Scotland's rural population during William Adam's lifetime it would have been unthinkable that the word 'architecture' could be applied to their dwellings described in 1679 with Thomas Kirke's customary vigorous exaggeration:

> The houses of the commonalty are very mean, mud-wall and thatch the best; but the poorer sort live in such miserable hutts as never eye beheld; men, women, and children pig altogether in a poor mouse-hole of mud, heath, and some such like matter; in some parts where turf is plentiful, they build up little cabbins thereof, with arched roofs of turf, without a stick of timber in it; when their houses are dry enough to burn, it serves them for fuel, and they remove to another.[1]

The chief element of these buildings, the home-made product of the peasantry they housed, was a framework of wooden crucks, their lower ends raised above the damp earth on boulders or a stone base-course.[2] The walls were of turf, often alternating with bands of stones, clay,[3] or clayed wattle,[4] the roofs of turf or thatch.[5] These hovels did not provide much in the way of comfort but their erection did not demand specialised skills and made use of readily available materials. Their cheapness and ease of construction were well suited to the poverty of their inhabitants.

The construction of churches, public buildings, and houses for landowners and merchants demanded a qualitatively different organisation. Materials had to be collected, often with difficulty and from a distance, and craftsmen had to be found and supervised.

The main walls of 'polite' buildings were almost always of stone quarried without much mechanical assistance, the chief instruments used being wedges to produce a cleavage line and small charges of gunpowder to blow the stone from the rock-face.[6] Inadequate pumps meant that flooding of the quarries was a constant problem. Sometimes stone could be re-used from an existing building. The contract for alterations to Cawdor Castle in 1699 provided that the masons were first:

> to cast down the litle tower of Calder to the very foundation if need be, and to preserve the stones as heall as they can, especiallie the hewen work . . . [7]

Often a local quarry could be used or opened. When the rebuilding of Inveraray Castle began in 1745 twenty-eight quarriers were employed in three local quarries.[8] Sometimes a mixture of local stone and stone brought from a distance was employed. When William Adam paved the hall at Yester he used stone from a nearby quarry at Whittingehame and stone brought from Dalgety in Fife.[9] At another of his major buildings, Duff House near Banff, the two main fronts were faced with Morayshire stone, the sides with stone from South Queensferry in West Lothian.[10] Unusual in the distance it travelled was the stone from Norrköping in Sweden bought by the Edinburgh developer Thomas Robertson in 1682, but the total length of the journey was generally less important than the nearness or farness of quarry and building site from harbours.[11] The stone brought from Dalgety to Yester in 1730 was shipped across the Firth of Forth to Port Seton,[12] the boatmen receiving thirty pints of ale for their two trips.[13] The Morayshire stone used at Duff House came from a quarry 'near to the Sea side' and the Queensferry stone was 'Transported to Banff at no very great Charge by the means of Boats or Barks that are frequently going from this firth [of Forth] to the North to fetch meall . . . '[14]

Lime for mortar was generally quarried locally and, until the late eighteenth century, burnt in primitive but cheaply constructed horizontal or clamp-kilns built of turf, earth and field-stones and fired by peat, charcoal or coal.[15] The lime used in repairs at Dunvegan Castle on Skye between 1707 and 1717 was produced from shells brought from Barra and burnt over peat fires.[16] The lime for work at Yester in 1705-6 and 1712 was bought from neighbouring farmers.[17] When William Adam reconstructed Brunstane House for Lord Milton in 1736 twenty cart-loads of limestone were supplied, with the promise of another twenty if wanted, from Carberry about five miles away.[18] Clearly here the lime was to be burnt on site as it was at Castle Grant in 1753 where the mason contracted to 'wien and buren the Lime and Souer the Sem'.[19] However, when Tarbat House in Easter Ross was reconstructed in 1688 the lime was sent from Edinburgh.[20]

Brick seems to have been first used as a building material in Scotland in the construction of the Cromwellian Citadel at Inverness in 1652–6. Its next recorded use is for the construction of office houses and garden walls at Megginch in Perthshire in 1707.[21] Doubts about its availability and the availability of bricklayers are clear from a letter of 1710 in which Lord Yester, then in London, advised his father about the building of Yester House:

> It is every bodys opinion here y[t]. ye partition walls should be of brick if it can be got. And I am very much for it tho it should cost some more money if ye brick can be got made & there be workmen y[t]. can build with brick.[22]

In 1718 when the army barracks at Fort Augustus were built of brick,[23] the surnames of George and John Ryalton (Railton), the brickmakers and bricklayers responsible, suggest that they were English.[24] Certainly brick was not in common use when Defoe visited the Marquess of Annandale's house at Craigiehall near Edinburgh in 1724:

> And here I observ'd his Lordship was making Bricks, in order to build Walls round his garden; a Thing hardly to be seen in *Scotland*, except there. On the other Hand, it is for want of Brick Walls that the Wall-Fruit in *Scotland* does not thrive so well there as it would otherwise do . . .[25]

The main use of brick in the early eighteenth century was for the internal facing of stone walls and for partition walls. In 1745 William Adam advised its use in the proposed addition to Rosneath in Dunbartonshire:

> As there is Clay here that will answer for making of Bricks & that it is thought propper to line the Insides of the Walls of the new rooms therewith, which is much dryer than Stone, & consequently may have the use of these rooms the sooner.[26]

At Rosneath, as at Inveraray at the same time, the clay was dug locally and a brickmaker brought in for the work, but commercial brickworks did exist.[27] Perhaps the first was that founded by William Adam and William Robertson at Linktown of Abbotshall in 1714.[28] By 1743 bricks were also being made at Leith.[29]

The commercial manufacture of bricks was usually associated with the making of pantiles. Although an Act of Edinburgh Burgh

Council in 1677 stipulating that new buildings were to be roofed with 'sclait or tyll' implies that tiles were in use by the late seventeenth century, they do not seem to have been common before 1700.[30] In Fife the first recorded example of a manse or its outbuildings being covered with pantiles dates from 1708.[31] Thereafter they were frequently used in place of thatch or turfs. In 1722 William Adam was paid £1 16s. for supplying a hundred tiles for the office houses at Aberdour Manse.[32] Pantiles were also imported from England and apparently Holland. In 1732 an advertisement in *The Caledonian Mercury* announced the arrival at Leith of pantiles from Stockton, 'being better than any made in this country'.[33] Eleven years later the Leith tile works boasted that their pantiles were 'as good as any ever came from Holland',[34] and Aberdeen tiles were proclaimed 'every way as good as the Dutch'.[35]

Houses of any pretension were roofed with slates. In the seventeenth century these had often been not true slates but sandstone slabs ('grey slates') whose quarrying provided a local industry at Carmylie in Angus.[36] The eighteenth century's grander buildings were covered with true slates ('blue slates') coming from a number of quarries. In 1663 'the fynest blew sklaite of stobo hill' was brought from Peeblesshire to Yester.[37] For the rebuilding of that house in 1714 a boatload of slate came from Kames Bay in Bute.[38] Eighteen thousand slates costing £228 were supplied to Cawdor Castle from Daltullich in 1716.[39] By far the most important source of slate in early eighteenth-century Scotland was the island of Easdale in the Firth of Lorne. Here slate had been quarried since the seventeenth century, at first from the exposed strata by the shore into whose cleavage seams were driven oak wedges which expanded when the tide came in and so detached the rock. Later, the slate was blasted out with gunpowder.[40] Sizes of slates could be firmly specified as in 1719 when the Edinburgh merchant Patrick Stewart contracted to deliver to Newhailes:

> The Number of Twenty Thousand blew sclaits or Scailzie of the dimensions following Viz The Shortest to be Ten inches long and Six Inches broad at the lower end with four easing sclaits to be hundred, The forsd easings not to be under eight Inches broad & fiveteen Inches long . . .[41]

In 1752 after 'sundry Complaints have been made, that the Easdale Slates are *too small* in Size', the Easdale quarry announced that slate would be supplied in lots of 1,000 composed of slates of four sizes.[42]

Lead was used for pipes, gutters, roof flats and flashings. Its mining on a large scale was begun in about 1590 at Leadhills in Lanarkshire. By the mid-seventeenth century these mines employed about fifty workmen to extract 300–400 tons of ore each year from as deep as twenty-four fathoms.[43] By the end of that century one of Scotland's very few roads fit for wheeled traffic was the cart-road from Leadhills to Leith.[44] In 1675 a second large mine was opened at Wanlockhead in Dumfriesshire and soon after mining began on Islay. By 1720 the industry probably employed 200 workmen and had an annual production of 1,500 tons of ore. At first charcoal was used for smelting but its replacement by the much more widely available peat meant that most of the ore could be smelted at the mines and only smelted bars had to be transported for any distance. By about 1720 the price of a smelted bar was £12–£13 a ton,[45] but substantial amounts were used for building as at Yester where in 1730 the Marquess of Tweeddale bought 411 bars, 2,876 stone and nine pounds of lead from Wanlockhead.[46]

In November, 1686, Alexander Hay advised the Earl of Tweeddale not to delay in buying nails 'which is a great materiall in yor. building, & at this time the pryses are low.'[47] Country forges were common, the smiths largely occupied with the shoeing of horses and the repair of agricultural implements, but larger-scale production of ironmongery also developed in the early eighteenth century. By 1723 there was an iron mill at Achray near Aberfoyle and a forge of some importance at Dalkeith by 1730.[48] Some Scottish iron ore and scrap iron was smelted,[49] but much of the raw material was imported from Sweden in the form of iron bars ('gads'), about 1,000 tons being shipped each year between 1660 and 1707.[50]

Wood was an essential building material, both for its place in the finished structure and for scaffolding during construction. When William Adam signed a contract with the Marquess of Tweeddale for the reconstruction of Yester in 1729 it was stipulated that the Marquess was to cut 'Two Rows of the firr Trees now growing in the Garden' for scaffolding. He was also to allow Adam three or four trees from the park for making a 'hand or horse machine', to hoist materials to the roof of the house.[51] At Yester wood was abundant since the first and second Marquesses of Tweeddale were reputed in 1724 to have 'planted above 6000

Acres of Land all full of Firr-Trees; and that, where-ever it was found that any Tree fail'd, they were constantly renew'd the next Year'.[52] Their example had been followed by other Lothian land-owners so that Defoe reported:

> . . . you hardly see a Gentleman's House, as you pass the *Louthians*, towards *Edinburgh*, but they are distinguish'd by Groves and Walks of Firr-Trees about them; which tho' in most Places they are but young, yet they shew us, that in a few Years, *Scotland* will not need to send to *Norway* for Timber and Deal, but will have sufficient of her own, and perhaps, be able to furnish *England* too with considerable Quantities.[53]

Besides the new plantations of the late seventeenth and early eighteenth centuries there was a large amount of natural woodland in some areas. In the western Highlands the 'Young' Lochiel was managing his woods as a commercial asset in the years before the 1745 rising.[54] In north-east Ross in 1688 the Viscount of Tarbat expected wood for his additions to Tarbat House to be found locally, writing to his son:

> I expected that there was timber enough at Tarbat for jeasts and rooff and windowes: but now that much of that is gone, cast up what will be necessar for floors and rooff, and try if yee can be provided of all att home ether be Bellnigown, Inercharron, or Alexander Ross, and at what rates . . . Or yee conclud, try if Sir James Calder will furnish yow; perhaps he may, both better and cheaper.[55]

But mature home-grown timber was not of itself sufficient to satisfy Scotland's demand. For the building of Duff House which he began in 1735 Lord Braco:

> provided himself partly from his own woods in Braemarr where there are very fine trees which he caused to be flotted down the river Dee to Aberdeen and from thence brought about to Banff and partly by Cargoes which he caused to be Imported for his own house from Norway . . . [56]

Between 1680 and 1686, 30 per cent of ships arriving in Scottish ports from overseas came from Norway and their main cargo was wood. In the decade 1685–95 Scotland imported an average of about 360,000 pieces of Norwegian timber, mostly as sawn fir planks ('deals') but some as great baulks of roughly shaped fir ('trees').[57] In 1686 the Earl of Tweeddale paid the Leith skipper Matthew McCallum for bringing a cargo of 2,200 deals and 218 'cuts' from Langfjord,[58] and in 1716 John Campbell of Cawdor bought 490 feet of 'Noroway dealis' at a price of £190 and forty 'Noroway double deals' costing eight shillings each.[59] Wood for panelling, whether pine or oak, was often imported. Sixty 'Sweeds daills [Swedish deals]' were used to panel two rooms at Newhailes in 1710.[60] Wood for the panelling and sash windows at Tarbat House in 1686 was expected to come from Holland,[61] probably serving as an *entrepôt* for a cargo from the southern Baltic which supplied eastern Scotland with oak,[62] as Ireland did the west.[63]

Every sizeable burgh had its timber yard (the 'houf' or 'bush') where wood was seasoned for up to three years, the merchants paying a small rent to the burgh authorities for the yard's upkeep.[64] The sharpness of competition for good quality timber is made clear by a letter to Lord Milton from his factor in 1730:

> This only goes to acquaint you that the 200 fine Deals I told you I had bespoke from Mr. Shireff can hardly be gott keeped in his Timber yaird[.] Yesterday Lord Somervile sent his wright Arch[ibald] Chessels who woud needs have them but as I had bespoke them for your Lo[rdshi]p Mr Shireff wou'd not allow them to goe at any rate, but he bids me begg of your Lo[rdshi]p to take them away out of sight as soon as possible, as it may disoblidge his Customers who want such when he Can't serve them.[65]

All these materials had to be transported to the building site. Unless this was actually in a port it was necessary to use carts drawn by horses or oxen. Often these could be provided by the landowner or his tenants. In 1722 Lord Tweeddale's grieve at Yester wrote to his counterpart on Tweeddale's nearby estate of Pinkie:

> ... I wad have you to see if the carts at Pinky can trist [tryst] against Saterdays morning to Cary the deals that is at Fisheraw to Yester it will take 12 Carts to cary them I wad think that wad be a good day for then the horses geting the sabath days Rest after . . . [66]

In making preparations for work at Rosneath in 1745 William Adam stated that:

It is thought thrie Carts with 2 horses & a man to each Cart will be sufficient to carry all the stones from the shore to the work, also Lyme, Sand, Timber Bricks & Water.[67]

He went on to ask if the Duke of Argyll would provide these out of his own resources or if they were to be found some other way.

An indication of the organisation required to get a large-scale building operation under way is given by the memorandum William Adam produced in 1746 at the beginning of operations for the building of Inveraray Castle. Stone for rubble work was expected to come from two local quarries, lime from a third, and most of the ashlar from a fourth, the Creggans quarry, all on the opposite side of Loch Fyne to the building site. At Creggans eight quarriers or pickmen assisted by eighteen to twenty labourers were to be set to work. The quarriers had to be provided with all their tools ('mills, wedges, picks, mattocks, Crow Irons, Spades, Shovels, Wheell barrows, & Hand barrows') whose ironwork was to be bought ready-made in Glasgow, the wooden parts being produced at Inveraray. Cart roads were to be made from the quarries to the shore of Loch Fyne to which the stone was to be carried in three carts, each provided with two horses and a carter. A hut had to be built to house the men, as had stabling for the horses. To superintend the quarrying work Adam recommended the appointment of two overseers.

Across Loch Fyne from the quarries and near the site of the castle, sand was to be dug to make mortar when mixed with lime, the water for whose slaking was to be piped from springs. A bricklayer was to be employed to make bricks from local clay. At the site itself were to be at least eight carts, sixteen horses and eight carters. These carts were to be made and kept in repair by a cartwright assisted by a smith who would also shoe the horses, make and mend workmen's tools and, in any spare time, make nails, although 'some barrels of different kinds' of these were to be procured immediately from Glasgow. For wood, pine was to be cut locally but foreign pine and oak were also to be imported. For certain parts of the ashlar-work stone was to be brought from Arran or the Comeries. Adam suggested the purchase of a 'gabert' or sailing barge and hire of a crew:

The imployment of this Vessel & Crew will be, to carry Coall from Clyde for burning of Lyme Stone & Bricks, to Carry Lyme Stone from the head of the Loch to Inveraray, to carry Bricks if any are made on the side of the Loch, to carry Free Stone from the Shore at Craigen to this place, & to bring what Free Stone may be needed from Arran or the Comeries.

Even with the purchase of this boat Adam thought it would be necessary to hire other boats to carry goods to the work from time to time.[68]

The number of workmen employed on a building could be very large. On one day in 1684 the master of work at Drumlanrig Castle was superintending thirty-one masons, nine wrights, two smiths, six quarriers and fifteen barrowmen.[69] That number was exceptional but the influx of a sizeable workforce could strain local resources. When Duff House was being built in the 1730s the masons complained 'That those with Whom they Were Boarded Would Not Support them Unless they Procured Meall for themselves',[70] and Lord Braco was forced to sell them oatmeal from his own girnel at a cheap rate, an expedient followed at Inveraray.[71] Day-to-day supervision of work could be demanding. In 1723 when large office pavilions were being added to Dupplin, the architect James Smith lived on site.[72] Much more commonly superintendence was left to overseers who did not always prove conscientious. The overseer of the quarries at Inveraray:

> kept a suttlery at the Quarry and sold great Quantity of spirits, so that the men were very often Drunk at his house, when they should have been at work and he himself Encourageing them to this practice . . . [73]

A different problem was caused by the overseer at Castle Grant in 1753 who, 'as he is very sober, & uneasie that he should be brought in the way of drinking in the publick house, incase he lys there', asked to be lodged in the castle itself.[74] But whether they were given to excessive drinking or embarrassed sobriety, it was on his overseers that William Adam largely depended for his work as an architect-contractor. In his lawsuit against Lord Braco in 1743 he testified that:

> Mr Adams being frequently imployed in Undertakings of this Kind had for many years past, trained up a Number of Young Men whom he keeped in constant pay and imployment, the most experienced

of these being imployed at a very high wage, as Overseers and Directors of the works as the Samen were carried on in different parts of the Countrey as he could not constantly attend in all these different places himself and having thus the Choice and imployment of his own Servants he was answerable for their Skill and fidelity.[75]

Chapter 3

CRAFTSMEN AND JOURNEYMEN

The craftsmen of the seventeenth- and eighteenth-century building trades were trained and based in burghs within whose boundaries the exercise of a craft was restricted to the members of the guilds or incorporations and their employees. This monopoly was guarded carefully. In 1705 the Edinburgh masons' guild ordered the arrest of 'any jurniman who shall be found jobing to any person w[ithi]n this brough without ane master',[1] and in 1716 the Culross incorporation of wrights fined and imprisoned William Pains for 'working the wright Craft within the priveledg of this brugh' without being employed by a freeman.[2] The justification for this restrictive practice was that it served the interests of both the consumer and the master craftsman as was stated in 1592 by the Act of Parliament which extended the craft monopoly to the suburbs of royal burghs:

> . . . the exerceis[e]s of craftismen in the subvrbis of the frie burrowis Is not onlie hurtful to all oᵣ souerane lordis liegis for the insufficie[n]cie of the work Bot als ministrattis greit occasioun to prenteis[e]s and s[er]vandis in frie burrowis vndewtifullie to leive their maisteris . . . [3]

Boys were bound as apprentices by indentures usually when in their mid- or late teens and lived in their master's household.[4] In Edinburgh, after 1685, apprentice masons were forbidden to marry.[5] The duration of an apprenticeship varied from craft to craft and place to place. In late seventeenth-century Glasgow apprentice smiths served five years 'and two for meat and fie' while masons and wrights served seven years 'and two for meat and fie'.[6] In Arbroath smiths had to serve 'six years, and another for fee',[7] but in Perth by 1746 they were bound for only four years.[8] In Lanark, masons and wrights had to serve an apprenticeship of at least three years,[9] in Culross wrights had to serve four years.[10] In both Culross and Lanark the master was forbidden to take a second apprentice until the first had served all but a year of his time.[11] Generally, having served his time, the former apprentice had then to work as a journeyman before he could be admitted to membership of the craft incorporation and so be allowed to set up in business on his own and himself employ journeymen. In both Culross and Edinburgh this period of paid employment was set at a minimum of two years.[12] Many craftsmen were content to continue as journeymen. Of those who did become freemen, most had worked for longer than the minimum period. Of thirteen masons who applied for admission to the freedom in Edinburgh between 1680 and 1725 only two had been journeymen for as little as two years and another three for three years while no fewer than six had already worked as journeymen for between nine and eleven years.[13] Other ways to attain membership of a craft incorporation were by birth and marriage. The sons and sons-in-law of members of the incorporation were eligible for admission without having served a formal apprenticeship or worked as journeymen. Never-theless they had to show themselves competent. In 1718 the Culross Incorporation of Wrights enacted:

> that no man . . . be admitted a freeman to heave pour to Imploy journamen or other unless he Can work with his oun hand and give sufisent evedence therof . . . [14]

Five years later the Incorporation refused to admit Robert Roland whose father had been a member of the craft, finding 'that he hath no priveledge in regaird he is no wright nor can perform as such'.[15]

Before admission to the incorporation the craftsman had to give evidence of his skill by producing an essay or test piece specified by the guild. Sometimes the standard expected appears to have been low. In Perth in 1749 the smith James Moncrieff was set to make 'four Horse Shoes & two Clicks for a folding bed'.[16] In Culross James Anderson was told by the wrights in 1728 to produce:

> one square Buffet Stool Eighteen Inches high Eighteen Inches in Lenth and Ten Inches broad . . . [17]

More demanding was Dougal Ferguson's essay piece of 1734:

> a Closs bed bound & Arched in the foreside all the rest to be plain to be finished with Architrive freise & Cornish they are to be raised pannells, the foreside is to be devided in three leaves . . . [18]

Edinburgh was Scotland's principal supplier of luxury goods and its craftsmen engaged in the building trades were aiming to supply work of a design and execution appropriate to their situation. Here the masons, wrights, glaziers, plumbers, slaters, painters and upholsterers were grouped together in the Incorporation of Mary's Chapel named after its meeting place in a former chantry chapel at the head of Niddry's Wynd.[19] The essay pieces recorded in their minute books show a level of ambition and sophistication to which the Culross wrights and Perth hammermen never aspired to climb. The glaziers' more recondite skills were probably little in demand after sash windows had supplanted fixed lights in the late seventeenth century but their freemen were still required to have shown an ability to make a leaded window of decoratively patterned panes in accordance with one of the plates in Walter Gedde's *A Booke of Sundry draughtes, Principaly serving for Glasiers*, first published in London in 1615–16.[20]

Early eighteenth-century landscape with classical ruins, Caroline Park House

The painters showed a more up-to-date spirit. Unsurprisingly a few early eighteenth-century essays were heraldic, like that set for Roderick Chalmers in 1709, the depiction of:

the Royall armes of Great Brittaine within a canepe armine &
doublet with crimson velvet poudered with Lyons pass & garden
& Lyons rampant floured delizes & harps alternative & Signed
upon the top with ane imperiall croun ushing out thereof The
Royall Standart of Great Brittaine . . . [21]

But from the 1680s the commonest essay piece for a painter was
a decorative panel, usually a landscape, intended to be placed in
panelling above a door or fireplace. The subject David Craufurd
was required to paint in 1686 sounds enjoyable:

> A peece consisting of three foote high, and four & a halfe foote
> Long, Composed of Landskips, Sea's & Ships, with the Shoare
> thereof; adorned with Finn & shell Fishes and they are to be done
> in all poynts, Conform to the patern & draught to be given him
> thereanent . . . [23]

Rather less crowded was Walter Melville's subject in 1717:

> . . . a peece of landskip with ane fountain & the figure of a
> sheepherd with a few cattell . . . [23]

Usually these landscapes were derived from engravings, as in the
case of Walter Gordon who had in 1744 to paint 'a peice of Land-
scop after Porrelle . . . conforme to a print signed by the deacon.'[24]
Engravings were also the sources for historical and biblical scenes
like 'the history of Susana and the elders' painted by James Norie
in 1709,[25] John Mark's 'peece of history Landscope after Ruben
van Orley' of 1718,[26] or David Cleland's 'History Landscope, after
Berghame [Nicolaes Berchem] conforme to a print produced and
signed by the deacons' ordered in 1735.[27] Specifically architectural decoration could be required. In 1738 Edward Burton was
told to decorate a window blind in the Incorporation's laigh hall
with:

> a Proportionable Niche with an Architrave round it in which he
> must Set a Vaus handsomely Enriched all Done in stone Colour
> in oyl . . . [28]

Six years later James Millar was to paint 'a pece of ornament after
Watteau in gold & green collours hightned with gold on a white
ground',[29] and in 1749 James Allan had 'To paint and gild a peic
of ornament after *Charpenteir*'.[30] Proof of the painters' skill in

depicting landscapes, history scenes or *trompe l'oeil* was almost always accompanied by demonstration of their ability in marbling and graining. When in 1707 Alexander Syme was ordered to produce an oil painting from an engraving, he had also to paint 'ane peice of Boyne marble on the one syde thereof and ane peice of Cedar wood Coulour on the other'.[31] A few months later John Warrander was to frame his scene in a margin of 'ane peice of Gilded Tortoise shell . . . on the one syde and ane peice of Calledonia Marble on the other'.[32]

The wrights' essay pieces were almost always pieces of furniture but after 1674 they were also required to draw a column according to one of the classical orders.[33] From 1692 the textbook sources for the orders were specified. In that year John Henderson and James Paterson were ordered to follow respectively the Ionic and Composite orders 'conform to' Palladio, James Buchanan to follow the Corinthian order according to Scamozzi and Thomas Rutherford the Doric order of Vignola.[34] From then until the mid-eighteenth century Palladio was by far the most common authority specified, with Scamozzi and Vignola mentioned occasionally and Vitruvius once.[35] In most instances this knowledge of the classical orders was clearly intended only for application in furniture-making, as with John Wyper whose wainscot press made in 1711 had 'a wholl intabulator of the Corinthian order after Palladio', but occasionally a wright was expected to design a building.[36] In 1697 William Shuel was ordered both to make a wainscot press and also:

> to designe ye gru[nd] draught of a house of sixtie nyne foots square hav[ing] a large lantren stair of timber & back stairs of sto[ne] having a good outer room dyning roome drawing roome & fo[ur] bed Chambers ye least beeing tuintie foot one way and hold a bed & dark Chamber & stooll roome having a good Closet and beds right pleaced and to draw the frunt three Storie high with regular windoues . . . [37]

Thirty years later George Cowan's essay piece was:

> *A modell of a house* in Wood consisting of nynty foots in lenth, and fourty six foots in breadth over the walls with ane breaking outward on both corners of the front, as also a timpany [pediment] The house to be three stories high, with Basse & cornish to it and rustick corners. And to make a Rooff to the same. The first story of the house to be foure foots below ground & Haveing stairs,

doors, chimneys & Windows regularly placed to the severall
storys. And the chimney heads to be of a proportionall hight above
the Rooff And ordained him to draw the draught of the ground plot
and second story with the fronticepiece . . . [38]

The drawing of plans and elevations of houses or the making
of models was an almost invariable part of the testing of an Edinburgh mason in the seventeenth century and for most of the eighteenth. A typical essay piece was that set for Henry Wilson in
1706, the making of:

ane double House in paisboard Consisting of Sixtie or Sixtie Six
foot of length over the walls and threttie six foot in breadth over
the walls three Story high with a Turnpyke And to place windows
Chimneys and other Conveniencies according to art . . . [39]

It is evident from the descriptions of these essay pieces that Edinburgh masons were expected to be competent to design and build
sizeable mansions, although few were as large as the one to be
designed by James Smith II in 1691, the model and drawings
showing:

Ane house of Two hundred & Fiftie Foote over walls every way,
being quadrangle, haveing ane pavilion in each Corner to be a
double house, of Fifty Foote over the walls all the Four wayes, With
a Court Consisting of ane hundred and fifty Foote square within;
with Convenient entries, scale staires, Chimneys, windowes,
doores and private passages, and the same to be divided in Convenient Roomes, Conform to such a building, and the walls to be
finished for a Convenient Rooffe and the said building to Consist
of three story hight . . . [40]

Less ambitious but far from small was the house to be designed
by John Archibald in 1710:

. . . ane house consisting of ane hundered foot in Length over the
walls Thirty Six foot of breadth over the walls Two jams from the
bodie of the House thirty foot each of them in length over the walls
and twenty foot of breadth with a Scale stair two turnpykes with
door windows & chimneys placed Conform to art . . . [41]

Smith's quadrangular palace and Archibald's U-plan house would
seem to have been designs for houses which would have suited

contemporary clients if they could be persuaded to undertake their building. Not apparently old-fashioned in terms of contemporary architecture, they do not however seem to have been notably progressive. Suggestive of a design in advance of the architecture of the day is the description in 1733 of Robert Bennet's model of a house of 120 feet by 80 feet:

> Haveing a halfe Sunk storie, with a Breaking on each front In the forme of a Demi-octagon, and a court stair leading to the vestible floor . . . [42]

Many craftsmen continued for much if not all their working lives as journeymen dependent for employment, if they were not to try to make a living by doing jobbing work outside the burghs, on the freemen of the incorporations. Building work was seasonal and journeymen might be laid off in winter and taken on again in the spring or early summer as happened in 1695 with the Edinburgh wrights Adam Brown, David Crocket and Duncan Ferguson who were hired at the respective rates of 10s. Scots (10d. sterling), 8s. 6d. and 8s. per day by William Baillie to work on the roof of the College.[43] Some masters could provide employment, as often for building country houses as for urban work, for a considerable number of journeymen. In 1721 James Smith complained to his friend and client John Mackenzie of Delvine:

> I am at present straitned in warping (as ye websters say) a web of houses for to keep 15 or 18 measons at work . . . [44]

In 1737 William Adam was employing forty-six masons and an overseer, himself a freeman of the masons' incorporation of Dunfermline, in the building of Duff House.[45]

The master made his profit from the difference between what he charged his clients for labour and what he paid his workmen. In 1743 William Adam explained:

> That the Journeymen Masons in Edinburgh have a merk [13 d.] per diem from the Masters whether working in Town or Countrey And that all the Masters have Sixteen pence and two thirds of a penny pr diem for their men from Candlemas to Hallowday And from Halloway [sic.] to Candlemas (being the winter quarter) the Men had ten pr Diem and the Masters a merk for them.[46]

In addition to this profit from construction charges, the contractor, if also a designer, might receive payment for plans and elevations. In 1741 William Adam was paid £315 for the 'plan and
estimate of the intended buildings at Buchanan', but to get
payment for professional services was not necessarily straight-
forward.[47] If the architect regarded himself as more than a mere
contractor he had to submit to the uncertain conventions of gen-
tility. That these might preclude businesslike dealings was made
clear by Lord Braco's explanation in 1743 of how he had regarded
William Adam at the time of the construction of Duff House:

> At these Severall visits made to the petitioner [Lord Braco] by Mr
> Adams to give his Councill and advice as ane Architect he lived
> during his Stay at the petitioners house and was by him Con-
> sidered as a person of a liberall profession and to be treated not
> like a Tradesman who was to give in a bill, but like a Lawyer who
> receives or a Phisician who pays visits in order to give their Advice
> who get their Fees or honourarys without presenting ane Accompt
> or giving a receipt . . .[48]

Chapter 4

THE BEGINNINGS OF CLASSICISM

George Heriot's Hospital. Drawing by Paul Sandby

In 1624 the Edinburgh-born goldsmith and banker to James VI, George Heriot, died leaving the huge sum of £23,625 sterling for the building and endowment of a 'hospital' or charity school in Edinburgh. A site on the southern edge of the burgh was bought in 1627 and in the same year Heriot's nephew and executor, George Balcanquhall, Dean of Rochester, produced a 'paterne' or plan for the building which was accepted by the Trustees.[1] Whether Balcanquhall's 'paterne' was an engraving intended to be adapted by an Edinburgh master mason or a detailed drawing

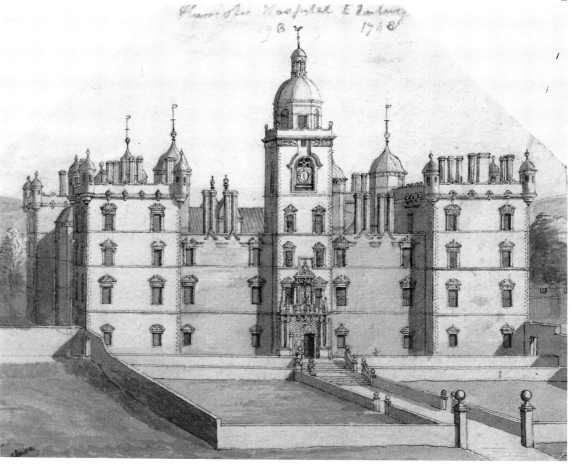

is not known, but the design of the school is clearly based on an engraved plan and elevation of a palace first published in 1575 in Sebastiano Serlio's *Seventh Book of Architecture*.[2] Serlio's plan of a quadrangular building with pavilion-towers at the outer corners and turrets in the inner angles and a tower above the central entrance was adhered to quite closely although of his elevations with superimposed orders of pilasters only their regular symmetry was observed, while the different treatment accorded to almost every window aedicule allowed masons to display their skills, and the octagonal chimneys and corner bartizans are respectively English and Scottish in flavour. But classicism of a type recognisable in continental Europe was not confined solely to the symmetry and composition. The Hall door was copied from Vignola's engraving of the principal entrance to the Farnese villa at Caprarola printed in his *Rules of the Five Orders* and the mannerist Chapel door's design is based on an example illustrated in Alexandre Francini's *Book of Architecture* of 1631, a source of inspiration also for the seventeenth-century monuments in the adjoining Greyfriars' Churchyard.[3]

George Heriot's Hospital, not finally completed until 1693, was the most ambitious building begun in Scotland during the first half of the seventeenth century. Its use of a classical plan makes it unique, although the adoption of isolated classical motifs was already commonplace among masons. Lairds' and noblemen's houses were usually built on an L- or Z-plan. Smart houses, like Winton in East Lothian built for the first Earl of Winton by William Wallace, Master Mason to the Crown, in the 1620s and Innes in Morayshire designed by Wallace's successor William Ayton about 1640 for the Laird of Innes, were both straight-forward L-plan buildings with a stair-tower in the inner angle but with pediments over the windows to show their owners' sophistication, their status being marked by such martial touches as gunloops at the ground floor. The predominant note is of an engaging compromise between the desire to hint at a classical education and the need to affirm baronial status. Most owners would have approved of the advice given the Earl of Lothian by Sir Robert Kerr in 1636 when alterations were proposed at Ancrum House:

> By any meanes do not take away the battlement, as some gave me counsale to do—for that is the grace of the house, and makes it look lyk a castle, and hence so nobleste . . .[4]

Craigievar Castle

Some houses erupted into a display of corbelling and turrets at
the top, most memorably the Aberdeenshire castle of Craigievar
completed in 1626 for a merchant who had invested in an estate.
The contemporary Castle Stuart in Inverness-shire is a sym-
metrical U-plan but the jambs are given wilfully different
treatments. Inside, these houses were essentially domestic,
generally with the ground floor given over to kitchen and storage
space, the first floor occupied by a hall or dining room with a
withdrawing-room and bedchamber leading off it *en suite*. The
floor or floors above were given over to more bedrooms.

The Cromwellian military occupation of Scotland between 1650 and 1660 was accompanied by the building of four citadels or forts (at Perth, Ayr, Inverness and Leith) designed in accordance with the latest European ideas of military architecture, polygonal in outline with triangular bastions to provide covering fire. For the Inverness citadel alternative designs were produced, the rejected one of a type illustrated in Buonanito Lorini's *Le Fortificationi* published in Venice in 1609 and in David Papillon's *A Practical Abstract of the Arts of Fortification and Assailing* which was put out in London in 1645, the accepted design taken from Robert Norwood's *Fortification or Military Architecture* of 1639. The architect responsible seems to have been the 'German ingenire' Joachim Hane. Another German, Hans Ewald Tessin, was responsible for the Ayr citadel.[5] While English and German experts on military architecture were working in Scotland, Scottish masons and architects were visiting England and the Continent. In 1652–3 John Mylne, Master Mason to the Crown and Captain of Pioneers and Master Gunner of Scotland under Charles I and Charles II, spent nine months in London as one of the Scottish Commissioners negotiating a Treaty of Union with England.[6] Of those who spent time on the Continent the most famous is Sir William Bruce.

Bruce was born about 1625–30, the younger son of Robert Bruce, owner of the small estate of Blairhall near Culross, a man of good family connections being the great-nephew of the first Lord Bruce of Kinloss and of Sir George Bruce of Carnock, and husband of a daughter of Sir Robert Preston of Valleyfield. Both Sir William Bruce's sisters were to marry earls.[7] Sir William Bruce may have attended the University of St Andrews in 1637–8 and in later years he showed a knowledge of Dutch, German, French, Italian and Latin.[8] It was as a political figure, engaged in some way with negotiations between General Monk and Charles II leading to the restoration of the monarchy, that Bruce is first properly recorded. In September, 1659, Monk granted him a passport 'to passe about his occasions on this side the Fryth [of Forth] & other parts of Scotland' before his 'returne to Holland' where the King was then in exile.[9] According to the account given in Sir Robert Douglas' *Baronage*, Bruce:

> was too young to have been very active in the troublesome reign of king Charles I. but no gentleman in a private capacity contributed more to bring about the restoration of his son, than this

sir William: Being of a fine address, he found means to get
acquainted with general Monk, to whom, 'tis said, that he painted
the distress and distractions of our country, and the glory that
would be acquired in restoring the royal family, in such lively
colours, that the general at last opened his mind to him, and
signified his inclination to serve the king; but that their measures
were to be carried on with the utmost caution and secrecy. These
joyful tidings sir William had the honour to communicate to the
king . . . [10]

Knighted soon after the Restoration, Bruce then followed a
political and administrative career, for much of the time as a supporter of the Earl (later Duke) of Lauderdale, the Scottish
Secretary of State until 1679, being Clerk to the Bills from 1660
to 1681, Surveyor General and Overseer of the King's Buildings

Sir William Bruce,
by Michael Wright

in Scotland in 1671-8,[11] Member of Parliament for Fife in
1669-74 and for Kinross-shire in 1681-2 and 1685-6,[12]
hereditary Sheriff of Kinross from 1675,[13] and a member of the
Privy Council in 1685-6.[14] The profits from these offices enabled
him to set up as a landowner, first at the Fife estate of Balcaskie
which he bought in 1665 and ten years later, on selling Balcaskie,
at Kinross. He was made a baronet in 1668 and later seems to
have had expectations of a viscountcy.[15] This successful career
was ended by his dismissal from office by James VII in 1686 and
Bruce's Jacobite sympathies made him a figure of suspicion to
James's successors. But if Bruce's political career ended in disappointment it had, nonetheless, enabled him to acquire a large
estate and obtain advantageous marriages for his children, his
daughter's two husbands being Sir Thomas Hope of Craighall and
Sir John Carstairs of Kilconquhar, his son marrying Lady Christian Leslie, daughter of the Duke of Rothes and widow of the Marquess of Montrose.[16]

Throughout his years of political office and after his fall from
royal favour Bruce acted as the architectural adviser and arbiter
of Scotland's Restoration nobility. In the earliest architectural
works associated with him he appears as a consultant or client
and it is doubtful how far he was responsible for their design. The
first house associated with Bruce was Leslie House, a palace built
for the Earl of Rothes, then Lord High Chancellor of Scotland, in
1667-72 by the King's Master Masons John Mylne and his
nephew Robert. The work at Leslie involved the expansion of an
existing house, apparently a sizeable L-plan, into a quadrangle,
the massively increased size providing accommodation for a state
apartment, a suite of rooms which could in theory accommodate

Leslie House
(Vitruvius Scoticus)

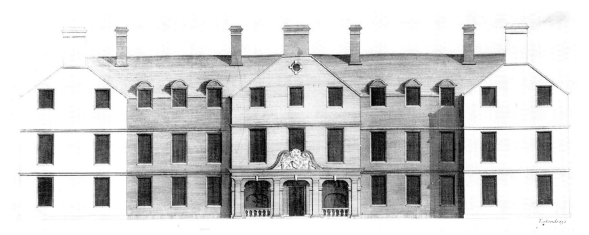

the King. Behind an arcaded loggia in the centre of the entrance front was a vestibule opening on the left into a great staircase giving access to the state apartment which began with a saloon followed by a drawing room, ante-chamber, bedchamber in the centre of the south front, and closet, essentially the same succession of rooms as was occupied by the monarch in his own palace.[17] On the other side of the great stair lay a gallery filling the whole north range which was by 1726 'fill'd with Paintings, but especially, of the great Ancestors of the House of *Rothes* or *Lessly* at full Lengths, and in their Robes of Office or Habits of Ceremony . . .'[18] Bruce was certainly named in the main contract for the work as custodian of the 'draughts & mapes [working drawings]' of the building 'For regulating theirof For the use of baith parties (until the said) work be finished' and was consulted by the Countess of Rothes about furnishings.[19] It is likely that the main principles of the house's internal planning were determined by him in his capacity as a man of the world conversant with the planning of great houses and palaces in England, Holland and perhaps France, which he may have visited during a foreign journey in 1663.[20] This likelihood is made the stronger by the evidence of his own house of Balcaskie whose enlargement he began in 1668. Here he converted the existing three-storey L-plan house into a U, filling its open centre with a two-storey block (probably flat-roofed with a balustraded parapet), a device common enough in mid-seventeenth-century Holland and introduced two years earlier in Scotland by John Mylne at Panmure. But the similarity to Panmure is external. Inside, Panmure contained a muddle of rooms, but at Balcaskie Bruce created a state apartment filling most of the first floor.[21] The main door in the centre of the front opened into a vestibule, paved as at Leslie with

Panmure House
(Vitruvius Scoticus)

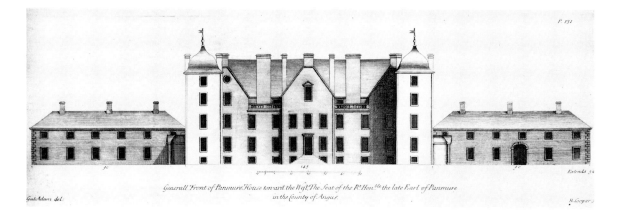

Generall Front of Panmure House toward the West. The Seat of the Rt Honble the late Earl of Panmure in the County of Angus.

black and white marble, with a grand stair on the left. The stair
rose to a first floor gallery behind which was the suite of state
dining room, drawing room, bedchamber and closet. The rooms
in which Bruce and his family lived and slept were mostly on the
floors above and below.[22] Just as ruthless in its alteration of a
house to conform to new ideas of planning, was the reconstruction of Thirlestane Castle in Berwickshire carried out between
1670 and 1682 by Robert Mylne under Bruce's direction.
Thirlestane was the principal Scottish seat of Bruce's political
patron, John, Duke of Lauderdale, Secretary of State for Scotland,
whose grandfather had built the existing house about a century
before. The sixteenth-century house was a long thin rectangle, the
side walls broken by a procession of turrets, the gable ends
gripped by drum towers. The ground floor was given over to
vaulted cellars and stores, the principal rooms being on the first
floor. The late seventeenth-century remodelling created two great
apartments, one for the Duke and Duchess of Lauderdale, the
other a state apartment. To achieve this, office ranges, one containing kitchens, the other stables, were added to the north-west
and south-west, thus freeing the main block's ground floor from
its cellar and storage purpose. At the same time tall rectangular

Thirlestane Castle.
Plan of ground floor
(Theatrum Scotiae)

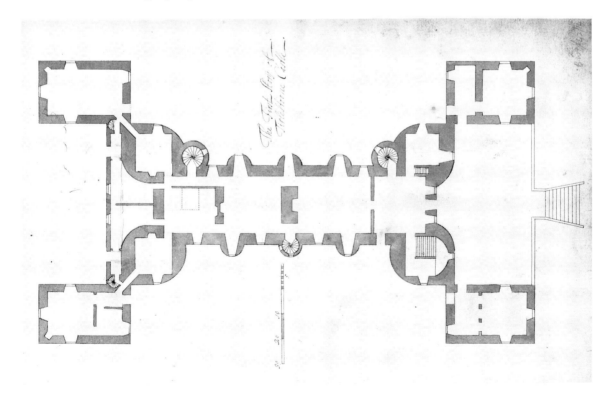

Palace of Holyroodhouse pavilions, the north containing a chapel, were built against the western drum towers. Between these was made a terrace approached by a flight of steps from an outer court leading to the new aediculed west door which replaced the original main entrance in the south front. From this door opened a vestibule behind which stretched an enfilade of new rooms (dining room, drawing room, bedchamber and closets) which formed the Duke and Duchess's apartment. In the northern drum tower, directly accessible from the vestibule, was placed a new grand stair to the identically planned but more lavishly decorated first floor state apartment.[23]

Bruce's early architectural career reached its climax with the virtual rebuilding of the royal palace of Holyroodhouse at Edinburgh. Except for its west range and the Abbey Church at the north-east corner the medieval palace had been wrecked by fire in 1650. In 1670 the Government ordered the expenditure of £30,000 on the repair of Holyroodhouse and Stirling Castle,[24] and it was to superintend this work that in 1671 Bruce was appointed Surveyor-General and Overseer of the King's Buildings in Scotland, a revival of the old office of Master of Work to the Crown vacant since 1668 but under a new title and with the salary trebled to £300.[25] Letters to Bruce from the Duke of Lauderdale make clear that the prime architectural responsibility for the

work at Holyroodhouse was Bruce's, although the plans seem to
have been drawn by Robert Mylne who signed the contract for
the mason work on 27 July, 1671.[26] After the King's disapproval
of a muddled scheme which would have provided three principal
apartments (presumably for the King, the Queen and the Lord
Commissioner to the Scottish Parliament), Bruce provided an
admirably lucid plan for two principal apartments on the first
floor. The King's apartment began at the state stair in the south-
west corner and progressed along the quadrangle's south and east
sides with a guardhall followed by a presence chamber, privy
chamber, ante-room and bedchamber (the grandest of these state
rooms and placed in the centre of the east front) and closet, with
the dressing-room, garderobe and page of the backstairs' room
behind. The Queen's apartment ran from the state stair along the
west range, the ante-chamber and bedchamber in the sixteenth-
century north-west tower being those formerly used by the King.
These two apartments were linked by a gallery along the north
range. Externally, the composition and design, which balanced
the north-west tower with a new south-west tower of the same late
Gothic character with a formal range between, its central
entrance topped by a Baroque crown, was thoroughly French.
Inside the courtyard and on the east front to the garden the elevations were treated with superimposed orders of pilasters, again
of French derivation.[27]

At the same time as Holyroodhouse was being built Bruce was
engaged on additions to Lauderdale's houses at Brunstane and
Lethington (now Lennoxlove). He also, in 1671 and 1675,
designed gates for Lauderdale's English seat of Ham House which
was then being remodelled by William Samwell with whom
Bruce was very probably brought into contact.[28] It was the
compact piend-roofed Anglo-Dutch type of house introduced to
England by Hugh May and Sir Roger Pratt which Bruce used as
his model in 1676 for his first country house built anew rather
than being remodelled or enlarged. That was Dunkeld House in
Perthshire to which Moncreiffe House of 1679 was so similar that
it must be assumed to have been also designed by Bruce.[29]

In 1686 Bruce began a new mansion for himself on his recently
purchased estate of Kinross. Here the standard English house of
the day was clothed in French dress. Kinross is a severe ashlar-
faced block with a slightly recessed centre, but the basement's
masonry is channelled in the French manner and the tiny
attic windows are squeezed between the main cornice and the

Kinross House   projecting eaves. At the ends are very widely spaced Corinthian pilasters, their distance from each other probably inspired by Bernini's first project for the Louvre illustrated in *Le Grand Marot*.[30] The roof's tall cupola had been the standard appendage of English houses since Sir Roger Pratt's design of about 1650 for Coleshill. Coleshill's plan may well have influenced that of Kinross. They are very similar except that at Coleshill the main stair was placed in the entrance hall while at Kinross it is sited to the left, and that at Coleshill there was on each of the principal floors one room (a ground floor great parlour and a first floor great dining chamber) behind the hall, at Kinross there were two unequally-sized rooms. These differences result from the provision at Kinross of a first floor state apartment. Consequently the space occupied in the centre of the front at Coleshill by the upper part of the stair-hall was required at Kinross for Bruce's 'Great Dyning roome' and the place of Pratt's Great Dining Chamber behind was occupied by the state apartment's withdrawing room and antechamber.[31] Bruce's loss of office in 1686 apparently

The Court Front of Harden House in the County of Teviotdale. Extends 101 feet

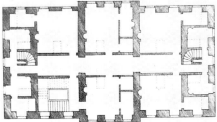

Plan of the Attick Story

Mezzanines over the Closets

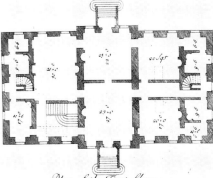

Plan of the First floor

Mezzanines over the Closets

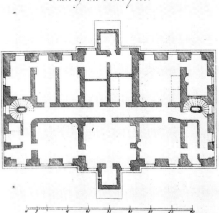

Plan of the Cellar Story

Sr. Wm. Bruce Invt.
Wiil Adam delin

R. Cooper Sculp.

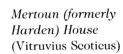

Mertoun (formerly Harden) House (Vitruvius Scoticus)

precluded the internal finishing of Kinross to its intended grandeur although in 1723 John Macky declared it 'by much the finest Seat I have yet seen in *Scotland* . . .'[32]

Bruce's designs for two other houses, Craigiehall in 1699 and Mertoun in 1703, were more conventional than Kinross, both being piended boxes with pedimented centrepieces, but Mertoun's overall rustication and Craigiehall's two-bay centre are of French rather than English derivation.[33] Very much grander and more inventive was Hopetoun House in West Lothian. Bruce's involvement began in 1698 when Tobias Bachop, the mason employed at Kinross, Craigiehall and Mertoun, contracted to build a house in accordance with a design 'made and Subscryved by Sir William Bruce'. The contract specified that such details as

Hopetoun House. Elevation and plan by Sir William Bruce (Vitruvius Scoticus)

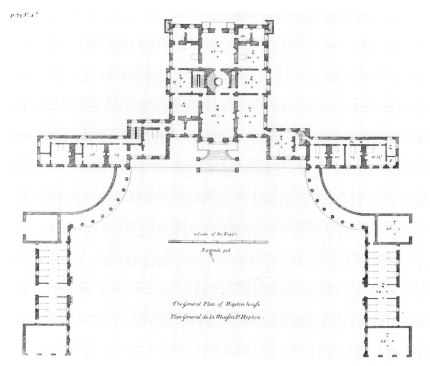

Hopetoun House. Plan by Sir William Bruce (Vitruvius Scoticus)

the rusticated basement and the window architraves were to be copied from Kinross or Craigiehall.[34] Another reminiscence of Craigiehall was the two-bay design of the side elevations' pedimented centres. The main front with a three-bay pedimented centre and piended platform roof topped by a cupola seems to have closely resembled William Samwell's elevation of Eaton Hall, Cheshire, built in 1675–82.[35] Hopetoun seems to have been completed in 1702, but four years later Bruce was brought back by the owner, Charles Hope, now aged twenty-five and recently ennobled as Earl of Hopetoun, to remodel the existing building and design large additions enclosing a great entrance court.[36] In the remodelling the main block's front was given overall channelled rustication and its three-bay centre acquired a ground floor arcade, perhaps derived from Louis Le Vau's Hôtel Tambonneau in Paris or possibly from Pieter Post's Maastricht Town Hall. The additions included large corner pavilions joined by boldly convex Tuscan colonnaded quadrants to the stable blocks each side of the forecourt, the ground plan perhaps taken from that of the terrace design of the Château de Marly. Inside the house, the plan of a Greek cross with a central octagon seems to be taken from Marly, but while at Marly the octagon contained the main 'salle', at Hopetoun it contained the stair with the garden parlour or principal family room behind. On each side of these centre rooms was an identically planned apartment comprising a drawing room, ante-chamber, bedchamber and closet, the northern apparently intended as the state apartment.[37] Bruce's scheme for Hopetoun remained uncompleted at his death in 1710 and eleven years later William Adam began another and yet grander remodelling of the house.

Contemporaries did not doubt Bruce's architectural importance. He was, according to Colen Campbell, 'justly esteem'd the best Architect of his time in that Kingdom [Scotland]'[38] and Sir John Clerk of Penicuik acknowledged him as 'the chief introducer of Architecture in this country'.[39] He must be credited as the major influence on the planning of country houses in the late seventeenth and early eighteenth centuries and as the populariser of the compact Anglo-Dutch type of house in Scotland. His own architectural vocabulary, eclectic but strongly French influenced, was used to produce buildings marked by a personal authority. But unlike Wren in England he was not a draughtsman of even passable competence. For the placing of his ideas on paper he was dependent on amanuenses. In 1697 when

the Earl of Melville was waiting for a design for Melville House,
Bruce excused his failure to produce one by explaining that:

> I have stayd constantly at home from week to week expecting
> either Mr Smith or Mr Edward coming here to extend the draught
> of your Lo[rdshi]p['s] house I have designd . . . [40]

Two weeks later he wrote rather more happily:

> I have painfully improven the draught I designed for your
> Lo[rdshi]p[']s house; and kept the bearer Mr Edward from
> morning till night close at work to extend the whole stories & the
> elevation of the fronts of ye whole, w[hi]c[h] were but ended this
> night late . . . [41]

The drawings for Holyroodhouse were by Robert Mylne, for
Kinross by the Episcopalian clergyman and architect Alexander
Edward.[42] But if Bruce's architectural skill was technically
limited, forcing him to rely on others to act as his draughtsmen,
that may itself have helped the spread among builders and other
architects of an understanding of classicism as more than an
anthology of motifs.

Seven years after Bruce's death Colen Campbell described
James Smith as 'the most experienc'd Architect of that Kingdom
[Scotland]'.[43] Smith, by then in his seventies, had been born the
son of a master mason who became a burgess of Forres. According
to his great-nephew Robert Mylne, he 'was bred to the Church,
but afterwards took to building'. Mylne also stated that he 'went
abroad to Italy and studied his Art', a statement partly confirmed
by Smith himself in 1715 when he stated that he had had a
'liberall education at schools and Colledges at home and abroad
and occasion to know the world by traveling abroad'.[44] That he
was regarded as entitled to be treated as a man of education is
clear from the title of 'Mr' which always prefaced his name, the
only other Scottish mason of the late seventeenth and early eighteenth centuries awarded this mark of respect being William
Adam. That he was competent in Latin is evident from a letter
he wrote to his friend and client John Mackenzie of Delvine, even
though he felt compelled to protest:

> Quod Mechanicus ausus sit rescribere Romano sermone cum (sit
> verecundia) haud vernacule bene scribere novit; nescio quo

Incentivo motus; nisi bene motum fuisset cui; et quod epistola
latina responsione ineruit ejusdem species . . . [45]

(That a mechanical has presumed to write a reply in the Roman
tongue when [in truth] he does not know how to write well in his
own, moved by I know not what prompting except it be his affection
and that a Latin letter has dragged out a reply of the same kind . . .)

That Smith was a skilled mason is equally clear. At the time of
his marriage in 1679 to Robert Mylne's daughter he had worked
under Mylne on the rebuilding of Holyroodhouse,[46] and when the
next year he was admitted to membership of the Incorporation
of Mary's Chapel, he produced as his essay piece the design or
model of:

> ane house of thrie stories heigh, of ane hundreth foot of Length
> and Fiftie foot wyde over walls, Being ane double hous with Four
> pavilions, each of ym tuelve foot diameter, with ane skaile stair
> eightine foot square And the stone work to finish pavilion way
> with ballasters Together with ane dorrick yett of ane different
> skaile . . . [47]

After his marriage he seems to have undertaken most of the
public commissions which would formerly have fallen to his
father-in-law as Master Mason to the Crown, beginning in 1680
with a bridge at Inverness,[48] and another over the Dee.[49] In 1683,
on the recommendation of the Duke of Queensberry, Smith was
appointed to the post of Surveyor or Overseer of the Royal Works
left vacant since Bruce's dismissal in 1678, a post he continued
to hold until the reign of George I although the annual salary of
£100 ceased to be paid after the Act of Union.[50]

Smith was architect or contractor for many of the largest
buildings put up in Scotland between 1680 and 1720. At
Hamilton Palace in the 1690s he built a long front, restrained
except for the pedimented centre marked by a giant Corinthian
order.[51] For the Duchess of Buccleuch in 1702–10 at Dalkeith
Palace he created a version of William III's Dutch palace of Het
Loo.[52] In 1701 he had begun a house which was to occupy both
him and William Adam for many years, Yester House in East
Lothian. Smith's design was for a beautifully austere piend-roofed
box of channelled ashlar with ogee-roofed pavilions projecting at
the corners of the entrance front. The main block's still
unfinished interior was described by John Macky in 1723:

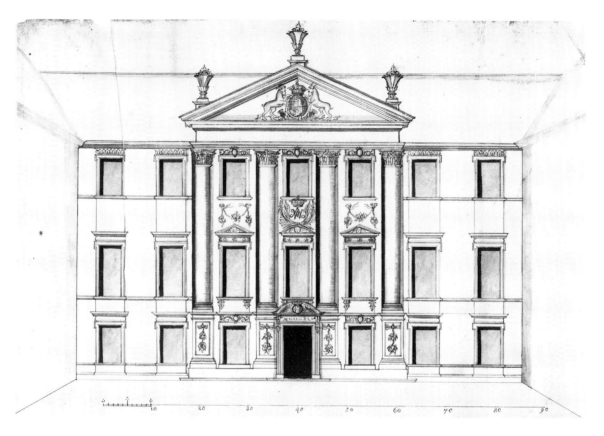

*Hamilton Palace.
Elevation by James
Smith, 1696*

You enter the Body of the House up six or eight Steps into a large Hall thirty-six Foot high, and behind it a Salon fronting the Garden of the same Height, and at top is a Gallery for Musick, which opens into both, exactly as at *Blenheim-House* in *Woodstock*. The Rooms of State, that run on each Side of this Salon fronting the Garden, are very stately, and of an exact Symmetry; and those from the Hall have a Communication with the Apartments in the two Pavilions. There is a mathematical Stone Stair, ballustraded with Iron, which leads you up to the Apartments above; but they are not yet so much as floored . . . [53]

Yester was the refined epitome of the compact box, but Smith's present reputation rests as much on his unexecuted designs as on his completed buildings. A number of his surviving drawings are studies on themes of Palladio including numerous designs for villas with centralised plans related to the Villa Rotonda. These passed into the ownership of Colen Campbell, the propagandist of Palladian architecture in England, and may thus have been influential in the development of the English Palladian movement.[54] However, the only one of Smith's executed works directly

John, eleventh Earl of Mar, and his eldest son, by Sir Godfrey Kneller

related to Palladio's influence is the mausoleum of Sir George Mackenzie of Rosehaugh at Edinburgh which he completed in 1691, the design closely derived from the upper storey of

Bramante's Tempietto di San Pietro in Montorio which Palladio
illustrated in the *Quattri Libri*.[55]

One of Smith's clients was John Erskine, eleventh Earl of Mar,
Secretary of State for Scotland under Queen Anne and later the
leader of the unsuccessful Jacobite rising of 1715 against George
I. Smith worked for Mar at Alloa,[56] and corresponded with him
about the repair of government buildings,[57] and seems to have
seen his own public employment as dependent on Mar's position
for he wrote to Mar in 1707 that:

> . . . I had rather your lo[rd]s[hi]p were to snuff at Court for many
> years for Smith can not spare youe from that place for I am afrayed
> yt there vould rise a Pharoch yt vould not knowe Joseph.[58]

Mar's own architectural career was entirely confined to paper projects produced during his exile from Britain after 1715,[59] but in the
years of his political power he was well established as an amateur
of architecture. He employed Sir Christopher Wren's workmen to
build a fountain at his English house in 1706,[60] and by 1709 James
Gibbs thought him 'very much my friend'.[61] At his Scottish seat of
Alloa he not only enlarged the house but laid out a huge formally
landscaped park which Macky in 1723 thought 'the largest and the
finest . . . of any in *Britain*; it far exceeds either *Hampton-Court*,
or *Kensington*'.[62] In 1701 Mar joined with other Scottish nobles
and lairds to send to London, Paris and the Low Countries Alexander Edward, an Episcopalian clergyman deprived of his parish
after the establishment of Presbyterianism in 1689 who had
become one of Bruce's draughtsmen and an architect and landscape designer in his own right.[63] Edward's commission was to:

> . . . view, observe and take draughts of the most curious and
> remarkable Houses, Edifices, Gardings, orchards, parks, planta-
> tions, land improvements, coall works, mines, water works and
> other curiosities of nature or art . . . [64]

Edward took this work seriously as evidenced by his letter written
to Mar from Le Havre in July, 1702:

> I have toiled for sight as much as I could & out wearied all I could
> ever ingadge & have searched for draughts both chops & Libraries
> & have spent almost 200 livers that way & purchased all the
> plangs of Houses gardens Ports Tombs doors Chimneys yea not

omitting Pulpits Churches & their Doms that my purse could reach or was to be sold & a good many perspectives & some pictures . . . I have bought a double of some good draughts of houses & diverse choise Gardens for your L[ordshi]p which exceed all thats to be gott at Lundon & I have purchased origenall draughts illuminat & drawn be the choisest designers of Gardens . . . [65]

Edward was more fortunate and probably harder working than the Marquess of Tullibardine who, when at The Hague four years later, wrote to Mar:

The best compleat prints I could get were Carolo: Maurat's works w.[ch] are here enclosed. I could get nothing yt. was entire of plans & veiws of gardens worth sending but versailes, villa Pamphillia & some other places in Italie w.[ch] no doubt you have being very common . . . [66]

Edward's death in 1708 seems to have caused a flurry of activity among Scottish aristocrats eager to get their hands on his collection of drawings. On 17 December the Earl of Panmure informed Mar that:

I have writ to Edr. to cause look after his draughts but I know not where they are to be found . . . [67]

In a letter the next day the architect and mason Alexander McGill mentioned to Mar:

. . . your desireing a share of the booty, if there be any pillfering about Mr Edwards sketches or draughts . . . [68]

By the opening decade of the eighteenth century architectural curiosity if not always sophistication was powerful in the minds of the Scottish aristocracy.

Chapter 5

ADAM'S EARLY YEARS

Williiam Adam was baptised on 24 October, 1689, in the parish church of Abbotshall just outside the royal burgh of Kirkcaldy on the Fife shore of the Firth of Forth.[1] His father John Adam was the descendant of a line of insignificant Angus lairds 'whom', according to William Adam's son-in-law John Clerk of Eldin, 'the spur of ambition had never roused into action' but who had 'transmitted a small paternal inheritance unimproved & unimpaired from father to son for many generations.'[2] In his *Baronage of Scotland* published in 1798 Sir Robert Douglas traced the family back to a Duncan Adam who lived in the reign of Robert I and whose son accompanied James, Lord Douglas, when he carried the heart of the Bruce on a crusading expedition to Spain in 1330. But Douglas is silent about the Adam family in the fifteenth century, his account of its members beginning again with a John Adam, 'a man of spirit and fortitude', killed at the Battle of Flodden in 1513, whose son Charles owned the small estate of Fanno (now Fonah) near Forfar by 1549. In the early seventeenth century Charles Adam's grandson Archibald sold Fanno and bought in its place the nearby estate of Queensmanor. Archibald Adam married Mary Hay, the daughter of a Montrose merchant, and their second son John became a mason who settled at the burgh of barony of Linktown of Abbotshall and fathered William Adam.[3]

In 1679 John Adam married Helen Cranstoun, one of the nine children of William, third Lord Cranstoun.[4] Her father had played an active though notably unsuccessful part in the mid-seventeenth-century Civil Wars, joining the Duke of Hamilton's invasion of England in 1648. After Hamilton's defeat by Cromwellian forces at the Battle of Preston, Cranstoun was taken prisoner, although soon released through the influence of his father-in-law, the Covenanting General, Sir Alexander Leslie, first Earl of Leven.[5] Three years later Lord Cranstoun was a member of Charles II's army which was routed at the Battle of Worcester where he was again captured and imprisoned for a time in the Tower of London,[6] before being released on parole and returning

to Scotland where his estates were confiscated.[7] Despite Colonel
Lilburne's suggestion in 1653 that these be returned to Cranstoun,[8] they were formally declared forfeit by the Act of Grace and
Pardon of 1654 although lands worth £200 *per annum* were
settled for the support of his wife and children.[9] At the beginning
of 1656 Lord Cranstoun had a commission from King Karl Gustav
of Sweden to raise a thousand Scottish soldiers for service with
the Swedish army fighting in Poland. Despite problems with
transporting these recruits the King was satisfied enough to ask
that Cranstoun's estates be returned to him. The request was
granted in June, 1656, but the lands produced an annual income
of only £596 and by then Lord Cranstoun's debts amounted to
over £10,000.[10] After the Restoration he failed to obtain much in
the way of financial relief,[11] and his only noteworthy action seems
to have been the killing of Captain Alexander Scrymgeour in a
duel in London in 1661.[12] This gallant soldier and impoverished
peer died about 1675, a few years before his daughter's marriage
to John Adam.[13]

The estate of Abbotshall was bought in about 1655 by Sir
Andrew Ramsay,[14] a past and future Lord Provost of Edinburgh
who was to become a Lord of Session in 1671 and a Commissioner for Trade in 1685.[15] The lands adjoined the royal burgh of
Kirkcaldy whose Council had complained in 1583 to the then
laird of Abbotshall about:

> the graitt abuse and hurt of the priviledges of this burgh be reason
> of ane multitude of unfrie craftismen dwelland on his ground, viz.
> Milntoun and Westbrig . . . [16]

The position of such craftsmen was regularised, although not to
the advantage of Kirkcaldy, by a Crown charter granted to Ramsay
in 1663 and ratified nine years later by Parliament, permitting
him to found a burgh of barony called Linktown with a weekly
market and twice-yearly four-day fairs.[17] In 1678 Ramsay allowed
the Linktown craftsmen to form themselves into two
monopolistic incorporations, those of the weavers and of the
hammermen who included smiths, masons and wrights. Before
he could take employment within the burgh a journeyman had
to pay 12s. Scots (1s. sterling) into the relevant incorporation's
'box' while an apprentice had to pay 24s. Scots at the beginning
of his indentures and a further 20s. for his 'upsett and Freedome',
the celebration of which was regulated by the stipulation:

that ther be no Feasting or drinking att the Speakeing or upsett
of any Freeman exceeding ane Merk Scots of expens . . . [18]

The incorporations added to Ramsay's original regulations. In
1702 the hammermen decreed that any member employing a
journeyman was to pay £1 10s. into the 'box',[19] and in 1710,
presumably after unseemly Sabbath behaviour, they ordered that:

> ther shall no hammerman goe into ye for seat in ye Church befor
> ye overseer and Boxmaister unless ye 3 Bell be runge

and furthermore, 'That non shall goe to ye forseat but who hath
beine maisters of ye treed . . .'[20]

Sir Andrew Ramsay's interests extended to salt panning and
coal mining. A Crown charter of 1671 granted him all saltpans
and their associated buildings within the burgh of Kirkcaldy itself,
together with the right:

> of digging and winning of coalls and panwood for serving the
> saids salt pannes in whatsume[ve]r pairt within the bounds of
> the lands of Abbotishall milnetoune comountie of Kirkaldie
> burrow aikers vnaikers wakerlands Bogie Bennoquhie Balsusney
> & easterdeanes . . .

This right was amplified by the provision that Ramsay was to have
within the area the monpoly:

> to have and make areholes sinks levells lenshers aqueducts water-
> drawghts waterworkes and others usefull and necessar for the
> wining and vpholding of the s[ai]ds coalls & coallhewghs alreadie
> wine or to be winne . . .

Coal surplus to the needs of the saltpans was to be used or sold
as Ramsay thought fit. Besides the extraction of coal he also
acquired the right:

> of haveing winning digging and away bringing of the claystone &
> lyme and other stones & necess[a]rs for the s[ai]ds saltpannes
> houss[es] and granaries therof . . . [21]

John Adam's name appears in the fragmentary surviving
minutes of the Linktown Incorporation of Hammermen as a
member regularly paying his quarterly dues, but of his work as
a mason the only record is of a few payments totalling £65 in

1695-6 for work at the nearby Raith House which was then being built apparently to a design by James Smith.[22] However, it is likely that he made a comfortable enough living as a builder-architect working in Linktown and its neighbourhood, perhaps involved with the construction of Ramsay's mansion house of Abbotshall, described in 1710 by Sir Robert Sibbald as 'a large and fine new house'.[23]

William Adam almost certainly attended the grammar school at Kirkcaldy which had been founded in 1582 to serve both the burgh and the surrounding rural area.[24] The school was taught by a schoolmaster assisted by a 'doctor'. At the time of William Adam's childhood the schoolmaster was paid a salary of £100 augmented by a capitation fee for each child, this fee being higher if the boy was studying Latin.[25] The school hours were from seven in the morning until five or six in the evening with hour-long breaks for breakfast and dinner on Mondays, Wednesdays and Fridays. On Tuesdays and Thursdays the school day finished at four and on Saturdays at noon,[26] but the boys were:

> discharged from playing in the Town, Church yard, in boats or ships, or anyways in the sea, as also from throwing stones, or playing with the carrock [playing shinty] on the streets, or from playing anywhere out of their houses after the eight o'clock bell at night, either summer or winter.[27]

The rules laid down on the appointment of a new schoolmaster in 1705 suggest that hard work of a strongly academic nature was expected, at least from the more intelligent pupils:

> . . . the Master shall be obliged to give theams [themes] to them who have learned their rudiments, once in the week; and twice in the week to them who have learned their first part; and thrice in the week to them who have learned their second part; and as many versions to each of these as the Master shall think fitt, and that every day all the scholars shall have copies to write by, betwixt ten and eleven in the forenoon. The Master also shall be obliged to cause them that are learning latine to have a repetition of all their weekly lessons upon what they have learned that week in their rudiments each Friday night, and a repetition of their authors each Saturday morning. And all shall dispute before twelve o'clock, and the victor be rewarded as the Master pleases; and that every quarter of a year they repeat the rules of the grammar, and revise authors that they have learned for that quarter, and every year at the visitation before the vacation, some in the first class

shall declaim orations before the Magistrates, Ministers, and
Elders, and all of them shall be peremptorily ordered to speak
latine to one another both in the school and out of it; and captens
appointed in every class strictly to observe such as speak english
that they may be corrected, and that such as learne English get frequent lessons in reading print and bills, and in their arithmetics.[28]

Nevertheless, when in 1707 a committee of the burgh council, its
members former pupils of the grammar school, met to consider
the appointment of a new schoolmaster, it was resolved that, 'in
respect that therefore this board is not altogether skilful of the
Lattine and Greek languages', help should be sought from the
Presbytery.[29]

William Adam probably left school in 1704 when he was fifteen
and then, according to his own account, 'he was bred a Mason and
Served his time as Such'.[30] He may well have trained under his
father who was certainly still alive in 1704,[31] although he seems
to have died some years later.[32] The only partial survival of the
records of the Linktown hammermen makes it impossible to state
when William was admitted to the freedom of the incorporation
but he is recorded as paying, or often failing to pay, his quarterly
dues from 1717 until 1734, by which time he was well-established
as a burgess of Edinburgh and when he seems finally to have
abandoned even nominal membership of the Linktown
incorporation.[33]

Apparently at some time before 1720 William Adam visited the
Low Countries and Northern France. This may have been intended
as a completion of his training as a mason-architect but is unlikely
to have taken place before 1713, when the Treaty of Utrecht
brought the war with France to a halt. Adam later mentioned this
trip when referring to the investigation he had made in the
1720s,[34] of the practicality of a Forth-Clyde canal, whose locks:

> I proposed to be of the same form as those at Ostend where I have
> seen ships raised up to the Canaal which leads betwixt Ostend &
> Bruges & so gone up to Bruges & discharged their Loading &
> returned the same way & let fall by the same sluices into the
> harbour at Ostend. I have likewise seen all those at Dunkirk where
> the largest men of war in France were raised into the Bason or Wett
> Dock.[35]

It was probably in reference to this foreign expedition that John
Clerk of Eldin claimed that:

Mr Adam brought a Modle of a Barley Miln from Holland, and introduced the making of Barley, and also the making of Dutch Pantiles
in Scotland.[36]

The mill mentioned can hardly be other than the one put up at
West Saltoun in East Lothian in 1711,[37] the first built in Scotland
for the production of pot or pearl barley and incorporating an
edge-running millstone and Dutch fannowers for winnowing,[38]
these last not used elsewhere in Scotland until after 1737.[39] But
the nature of William Adam's involvement with this mill's construction is unclear. The contract of 1710 between Henry Fletcher, as factor to his brother Andrew Fletcher of Saltoun, and the
millwright James Meikle stipulated:

> That the said James Meikle shall go to Holland with the first fleet
> that sails thither . . . and learn there the perfect art of sheeling
> barley; both that which is called French barley, and that which is
> called Pearl barley; and how to accommodate, order, and erect
> mills for that purpose, in so far as he can, with his uttermost
> industry, and recommendations given him.[40]

James Meikle fulfilled his obligations by going to Holland where
he and Andrew Fletcher seem jointly to have worked out the
design of the new mill.[41] When it had been built Meikle was
appointed master of work at the barley mill for life and bound by
a strict contract that:

> The said James Meikle shal discover the secret of the Milne to no
> person directly nor indirectly, nor give advice to any person for
> making one like to it or any part therof, conform to the oath
> already taken by him . . . And the said James Meikle when he is
> at home shal not allow any person whatsomever to enter into the
> Milne, except the Werkmen and those of Saltons or his Facters
> family and those of the said James Meikels own Family; and when
> he goes from home he shal leave strict orders with the Workmen
> to suffer no person to enter into the Milne . . . [42]

William Adam's part, if any, in the design or construction of the
Saltoun barley mill seems to have been only minor.

For John Clerk of Eldin's assertion that William Adam introduced the manufacture of 'Dutch Pantiles' to Scotland there is
substantially more evidence. On 8 May, 1714, William Adam and

William Robertson of Gladney signed a contract with Andrew
Ramsay of Abbotshall who granted them:

> the liberty and privilege of digging winning and away taking clay
> in any place within the Barrony of Abbotshall they shall think fitt
> for the Tyle and Brick manufactory to be erected by them in
> Linktown excepting always from the said priviledge the houses
> yards and parks belonging to the said M[r]. Andrew Ramsay with the
> fewers properties in Linktown, and also any part or portion of the
> said Barony that may any ways damage or prejudge the said M[r].
> Andrew Ramsay his milns or coal works.[43]

Mary Robertson, by
Allan Ramsay

The annual rent for this right to dig clay was to be 50 merks Scots and five hundred 'good & sufficient pantyles'.[44] By 1719 William Adam was named in a contract as the supplier of bricks for the building of Donibristle House,[45] and in 1722 he supplied a hundred tiles for roofing office houses at Aberdour Manse.[46]

William Adam's partner in the Linktown brick and tile works, William Robertson, was over thirty years his senior, having been born in 1656, the younger son of a Morayshire laird. By 1685 he was established as the bailie or principal factor on the estate of Margaret, Countess of Wemyss, immediately north of Kirkcaldy where relatively productive arable land was combined with extensive coal seams. In the same year he bought the small estate of Gladney near Cupar.[47] Five years later Robertson was appointed a Justice of the Peace for Fife,[48] and in 1696 he was rich enough to make the unwise investment of £1,000 in the Darien scheme.[49] In 1711, perhaps on retiring from management of the Wemyss estate, he bought land in Linktown of Abbotshall where he built Gladney House.[50] Besides investing with William Adam in the new brick and tile works, Robertson also took a lease on the Abbotshall coal mines.[51]

At Abbotshall on 30 May, 1716, the twenty-six year old William Adam married William Robertson's daughter Mary,[52] then aged eighteen.[53] Their first child Janet was born the next year and baptised at Abbotshall on 28 July, 1717.[54] William Adam, apparently the only one of his parents' children to have survived infancy,[55] was now established as a mason and co-owner of a brickworks, living with his wife and daughter in his father-in-law's house, by far the largest in the little burgh of Linktown.[56]

Domesticity seems to have accorded well with his temperament. Three years before marrying, William Adam gave evidence in a case brought before the Synod of Fife against a probationer-minister William Duguid, accused of unministerial behaviour. Adam recalled his part in one drinking session:

> that being in Company with Mr Dugud Glasmond & young Pitkennie in George Condie's house in Linktown they continued there till about nine of the clock at night & that he the deponent [*William Adam*] having said it was time for us all to goe home particularly for you Mr Dugud; Mr Dugud answered to this purpose Sutors [*shoemakers*] and Tailors counted hours but he intended to be merry with the company . . .[57]

Chapter 6

'MEASURER IN LINKTOWN' TO 'UNIVERSAL ARCHITECT'

On 20 December, 1720, the Presbytery of Kirkcaldy summoned a number of local tradesmen to report on the repairs needed to Abbotshall Parish Church. Among those summoned, one who did not appear was William Adam, 'measurer in Linktown'.[1] Adam's failure to comply with the Presbytery's request was not perhaps surprising since less than a month later, on 17 January, 1721, he signed a contract with the Earl of Hopetoun to build additions to Hopetoun House according to 'a draught to be fixed on by his Lordship'.[2] Four months after that, on 18 May, 1721, he was at Kelso to lay the foundations of the Duke of Roxburghe's new seat of Floors Castle.[3] At about the same time he was engaged in adding pavilions to the Earl of Breadalbane's Taymouth Castle and laying out the parterres and avenues of its landscape garden.[4] In January, 1723, he was simultaneously designing a house at Mavisbank for Sir John Clerk of Penicuik and an addition and landscape for the Earl of Stair at Newliston.[5] Over the next few years he was to reconstruct Lawers House for Stair's brother-in-law, build Dalmahoy House for Stair's brother, design a major reconstruction of Redbraes Castle for the Earl of Marchmont[6] and a new house at Mellerstain for the Earl's brother-in-law, George Baillie of Jerviswood, and build new mansion houses at Craigdarroch in Dumfriesshire and The Drum, and Arniston in Midlothian.[7] This intensity of activity brought the exasperated complaint from the Marquess of Annandale, very likely a putative client himself,[8] that:

> As for Adam's he has so many Real, and so many Imaginary projects, that he minds no body nor no thing to purpose.[9]

How and why did William Adam, the Linktown mason and measurer, become the architect and contractor for so many Scottish country houses in the 1720s? Any answer must owe much to speculation, but it is probably not coincidental that the emergence of William Adam as a major force in the architectural world came immediately after the apparent collapse of the architectural and contracting partnership of James Smith and

Alexander McGill, who had been responsible for almost every large building put up in Scotland during the past fifteen years. In 1719 Smith was dismissed from his post as surveyor of the new Highland forts being built by the Board of Ordnance, apparently because of delays in the erection of the first two for which he was contractor, and the building contract for the other two was given to Sir Patrick Strachan of Glenkindie,[10] leading Smith to complain:

> I was turned out of the service of the guverment after 36 years service without any malverse known or made manifest to me to make way for another who knows nothing of the mater (I mean Glenkindie) . . . [11]

Smith was now in his seventies and, willingly or not, seems largely to have retired from business, the only jobs of any size undertaken by him being the internal finishing of Yester House and the addition of office pavilions to Dupplin.[12]

Smith's dominant position as architect and contractor in the first twenty years of the eighteenth century can be attributed to his combining architectural knowledge, technical ability and enough capital to be able to supply materials and pay workmen without being dependent on immediate settlement of accounts by his clients. To these should be added his social position as the son-in-law of Robert Mylne who was not only Master Mason to the Scottish Crown but laird of Balfarg,[13] and himself the proprietor of the estate of Whitehill.[14] Socially William Adam could claim paternal descent from a family of lairds and raffish aristocratic connections on his mother's side. William Robertson, his father-in-law and early partner, had had a long association with the Wemyss family and was himself a laird. According to John Clerk of Eldin, Adam himself was:

> attended with a graceful, independent and engaging address which was remarked to command reverence from his inferiors, respect from his equals & uncommon friendship and attachment from men of the highest rank . . . [15]

Financially, William Adam seems to have been supported by the success of the Linktown brick and tile works and probably also by association with William Robertson's mining of the Abbotshall coal. His training as a mason provided him with a knowledge of construction, apparently widened by his examination of engineering works on his tour of the Low Countries and northern France. The extent of his architectural knowledge by 1720 is uncertain, although in the late nineteenth century his descendants' library at Blair Adam contained a sizeable collection of architectural works published before 1720, including books by Vitruvius, Palladio, Serlio, Scamozzi, Vignola, Fréart, Le Muet, Marot and du Cerceau.[16] It is probable that some of these had belonged to William Adam. In 1726 he certainly possessed at least an incomplete edition of Palladio's *Quattro libri* and the first two volumes of Colen Campbell's *Vitruvius Britannicus* and was eager to acquire illustrations of Inigo Jones' works.[17]

Several of William Adam's clients or prospective clients in the

Alexander, Lord Polwarth (later second Earl of Marchmont), by an unknown artist

early 1720s were themselves architectural amateurs. Among the subscribers to the first two volumes of *Vitruvius Britannicus* published in 1715 and 1717 were the Duke of Roxburghe, the Marquesses of Annandale and Tweeddale, the Earls of Breadalbane, Hopetoun and Stair, and Lord Polwarth (later Earl of Marchmont).[18] When, at the beginning of 1724, Lord Polwarth, then British ambassador at the Congress of Cambrai, perhaps anticipating his inheritance of his father's earldom and the estate of Redbraes, was considering how to remodel Redbraes Castle, he had worked out, at least in his mind, one scheme which included the provision of 'a magnificent Apartment 19 or 20 foot high' but sought advice from a number of sources. He wrote to his niece's husband Lord Binning:

> I hope this comes to you after you have got to London . . . I know not if you have brought up a Plan of Red-breas with you, if you have not I have writt to Sir James Hall to send you an exact one, of all the Storys and of all the hights, and when you get it pray advise with M^r. Campbell & M^r. Gibbs, and pay them for their advice, how to make it a good house, & get Plans from them, I'll do the same here [Cambrai] & if I can at Paris & will take the cheapest & best.[19]

As well as seeking plans from two of the most fashionable architects working in London, and from French architects, Lord Polwarth instructed his brother-in-law Sir James Hall of Dunglass to get a scheme from William Adam:

> You know this cannot be fallen about just now. But I would have you get L^d. Hopeton's Architect who no doubt is the best in Scotland and have His advice about makeing it a good House & let him be pay'd for his advice, then see if what I propose is practicable, & about what expence Tho I should be glad to have a Scheme from him & his advice first.[20]

In the event none of these schemes was executed and the only plans known to have been produced were those by William Adam, of whose design Lord Polwarth, by then Earl of Marchmont, told Sir James Hall:

> It pleas'd me very well especially since it did not oblige me to pull down the House nor alter the Situation. But to go to the expence of 5 or 6000£ for a House in the Country I think not adviseable.[21]

That Lord Polwarth, despite his eventual refusal to pay the cost of a grandly remodelled house, could approve Adam's proposals and regard him as an acceptable substitute for Colen Campbell or James Gibbs is a measure of how quickly this Fife mason had become accepted as Scotland's leading architect.

Patronage was pervasive in Scottish social and political life in the early eighteenth century and the second Earl of Stair, a strong supporter of the Hanoverian dynasty and ambassador to the French court between 1715 and 1720, was for William Adam, in the words of John Clerk of Eldin, 'one, who seemed by a sympathy of character to be peculiarly destined for the friend & Patron of such a man.'[22] William Adam himself wrote of Stair in 1724 that:

John, second Earl of Stair

realy if itt were in my power to prevent itt, I woud not disoblige
his L[ordshi]p, For he has been very Civill to me.[23]

Stair's significance in William Adam's career was more as a figure
of past and potentially future political importance than as himself
a munificent client. Of the effect on the Earl of his French
embassy, an eighteenth-century biographer stated:

> ... let it suffice, that in procuring Intelligence, and defeating the
> Projects form'd by the Partizans of the Pretender and other
> Enemies of the House of *Hanover*, that he spent his Fortune, and
> run himself considerably in Debt.[24]

After his recall from France in 1720 Stair spent the next twenty-
two years without Government office and partly engaged in agricultural improvement and the layout of the landscapes at Castle
Kennedy and Newliston,[25] on both of which William Adam was
engaged, but without the means to undertake any major building.
A patron whose support of the Hanoverians had brought him
much greater financial reward was the Earl of Hopetoun who,
when he first employed Adam in 1721, was receiving the huge
annual pension of £3,000.[26] Hopetoun's own architectural taste
had developed with visits to France and Italy[27] and was apparently further encouraged by his brother-in-law, James, second
Marquess of Annandale, who had visited Italy in 1717–20 and
brought back many classical marbles and engravings and over
three hundred paintings and drawings.[28]

Another of William Adam's patrons who had made an extended
Grand Tour was Sir John Clerk of Penicuik, described in 1725 by
the antiquary Alexander Gordon as 'Scotland's Maecenas'.[29] Born
the son of a baronet in 1676, Clerk studied law at Glasgow and
Leyden before suggesting to his father that he be permitted to
visit Italy to see its art and architecture since 'all the world are
bot imitators of the Italian masters'.[30] His two-year Grand Tour
during which he visited Germany, Austria and France as well as
Italy was begun in 1697.[31] At Rome he pursued the study of anti-
quity under the guidance of Chaprigni, music with Corelli,[32] and
architecture under a drawing master.[33] After Italy France came
as a disappointment:

> Paris was agreeable to me only for the conversation I found there,
> but was far from giving me that entertainment I had at Rome.

Every thing I saw seem'd only to be a copy from some great
Original I saw there, Houses, palaces, villas, Gardens, statues, pic-
tures, were all mean in comparison with what I had observed in
Italy.[34]

On his return to Scotland Clerk practised as an advocate at the
Scottish bar and sat in the Scottish Parliament as the Member for
Whithorn, a seat doubtless obtained through the influence of his
first wife's brother the Earl of Galloway. In 1708 he was made a
Baron of the Court of Exchequer.[35] His official duties were not
unduly onerous since the Court sat for only twelve weeks in the

*Sir John Clerk of
Penicuik, by William
Aikman*

year,[36] but the post provided him with the sizeable income of £500 a year of which he wrote in self-approval:

> I have always thought that my salary as a Baron of the Exchequer was publick money and a gratification I owed to my Country, and therfor I laid out the whole of it and some of my privat patrimony for the Improvement of my Country . . . [37]

These improvements consisted of planting and building on his estates where he also developed coal mines and excavated Roman antiquities.[38]

Clerk was very consciously an arbiter of taste. He acted as the Scottish clearing house for antiquarian information, himself writing works on Roman antiquities and joining in the fieldwork for Alexander Gordon's *Itinerarium Septentrionale*,[39] but his interests extended well beyond the antiquarian. In 1704 he advised the Earl of Hopetoun on gardening hints to be obtained from the works of Rossi and Falda.[40] In the same year he joined his father, himself a competent amateur architect, in helping Sir David Forbes with the design and construction of a new mansion house at Newhall.[41] Clerk's architectural judgments though could be erratic. In 1717 he wrote of Bruce's Kinross House:

> Whatever Sir William's talents were, the ornament of this house show nothing of them. Several gates and avenues are wrong placed, and the orders of Architecture are ill contrived and worse executed.[42]

Twenty years later he pronounced the same building to be 'in an Italian form . . . a very fine house.'[43] When he visited Chiswick House in 1727 he found it 'rather curious than convenient'[44] and on an engraving of another of Lord Burlington's works, the York Assembly Rooms, he wrote 'disproportionable.'[45] Where Clerk was consistent was in his insistence that houses should be fitted to their owners' station,[46] so that after a visit to Studley Royal in 1738 he sniffed:

> Here I saw a perfect superfluity of Temples, Groves, Parterrs, canals, and all other Embelishments, which seemed to become a prince more than a privat Man.[47]

Five years before on seeing Vanbrugh's Greenwich Hospital, 'one

of the most sumptuous buildings of the whole world', he was
moved to state that:

> One cannot but with indignation observe that the old broken
> seamen of England are lodged like kings and the kings like
> seamen, for the King's palace at St James's is no ways comparable
> to this hospital . . . [48]

Concern that a building should be appropriate to its owner's
status and activities underlies the instructions given to those
intending to build in his didactic manuscript poem 'The Country
Seat', where he distinguished between the royal palace, the 'house
of state', the 'house of convenience and use', and the villa.[49]

Of the houses William Adam began in 1721, Floors was
designed for John, first Duke of Roxburghe, Secretary of State for
Scotland and so in enjoyment of political office and its fruits. Roxburghe was described admiringly by his political opponent, the
Jacobite George Lockhart of Carnwath as:

> a Man of good Sense, improved by so much Reading and Learning,
> That, perhaps, he was the best Accomplish'd Young Man of Quality
> in *Europe*, and had so Charming a way of expressing his Thoughts,
> that he pleased even those 'gainst whom he spoke . . . [50]

The political and social position of this educated grandee
demanded something approaching Clerk's 'house of state' but
what was built was, although very large, relatively cheap, the
elevations all being of rubble rather than ashlar,[51] and the design
a curious mixture of the utilitarian and the sophisticated. The
house comprised a long three-storey and basement main block
from whose corners projected taller towers, those on the
entrance front joined by right-angled quadrants to two-storey
office pavilions. The piend-roofed pavilions were of the same type
as those being added at that time by James Smith to Dupplin
Castle but the main house seems to have been designed under
the direct influence of Colen Campbell. But if Campbell was the
influence it must mean that William Adam or the Duke of Roxburghe were in contact with him, since the Campbell schemes
to which Floors appears to be related were not published until
the appearance of the third volume of *Vitruvius Britannicus* in
1725. The general plan of a long thin house with boldly projecting
corner towers seems to be based on Campbell's unexecuted

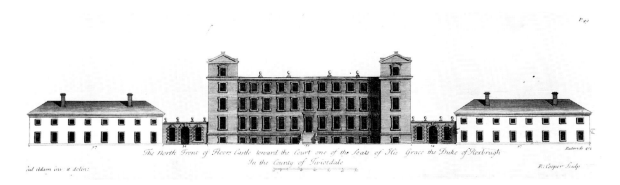

The North Front of Floors Castle toward the Court one of the Seats of His Grace the Duke of Roxbrugh In the County of Twiotdale

scheme prepared in 1720 for the remodelling of his neo-Palladian Wanstead House.[52] The treatment of the towers and, in general terms, of the whole front elevation, are derived from Isaac de Caux and Inigo Jones' south front of Wilton House of which Campbell had published an engraving in the second volume of *Vitruvius Britannicus* in 1717 and to which he himself turned at this time for his design for Houghton Hall in Norfolk, a show-house for the Prime Minister Sir Robert Walpole.[53] It seems more likely that Adam or his client were aware that Campbell was using Wilton as a starting point for his Houghton designs than that they came to the same source independently, especially since the projection of the corner towers occurs at Houghton as well as in the Wanstead design of 1720 but not at Wilton itself. At Floors the design of the towers' top stage was a fairly close copy of the Wilton prototype with pedimented windows under the overall pediment but the house's greater height and the omission of a crowning balustrade from the central range make it gawky in comparison with Wilton. The failure to provide any external distinction for the *piano nobile*, the windows of each floor having the same lugged architraves, precludes any identification of Floors with Palladian principles.

The internal planning, perhaps constrained by the incorporation of part of the previous house on the site, lacks the clarity characteristic of the work of Sir William Bruce and James Smith and which was to inform most of Adam's later buildings. Nevertheless, two hallmarks of William Adam's houses, the state apartment and a centrally placed library or billiard room on the lodging floor, are already present. The state apartment opening off the hall occupied the northern two thirds of the garden front and contained an ante-chamber, drawing room, bedchamber, dressing-room and closet. South of the ante-chamber was placed a great dining-room with a cabinet in the south-east tower. On the

Floors Castle
(Vitruvius Scoticus)

ground floor's west side were the principal family rooms. On the
first floor, a library or billiard room was placed above the hall in
the centre of the entrance front.

William Adam's creation of a ducal seat from the old castle of
Floors was only a part of the work undertaken by the Duke of Roxburghe who intended the house to be the centrepiece of a landscaped park beyond whose boundaries were to lie newly
enclosed farms and plantations. When Daniel Defoe visited in
1724 he found that:

> His [the Duke of Roxburghe's] House call'd *Floors* is an antient
> seat, but begins to wear a new Face; and those who view'd it fifteen
> or sixteen Years ago, will scarce know it again, if they should come
> a few Years hence, when the present Duke may have finished the
> Additions and Embellishments, which he is now making, and has
> been a considerable Time upon. Nor will the very Face of the
> Country appear the same, except it be that the River *Tweed* may,
> perhaps, run in the same Channel: But the Land before, lying open
> and wild, he will find enclos'd, cultivated and improv'd, Rows, and
> even Woods of Trees covering the champaign Country, and the
> House surrounded with large grown Vista's, and well planted
> Avenues, such as were never seen there before.[54]

Hopetoun had been built only twenty years before William
Adam began work there, and remodelled even more recently to
a design which Colen Campbell had published in the second
volume of *Vitruvius Britannicus*. It may have been that publication which caused the Earl of Hopetoun to feel dissatisfied with
his house, whose tall exposed roof was revealed as old-fashioned
when compared with the new English designs for houses whose
roofs were concealed by high balustraded attics.[55] An immediately practical reason for the enlargement of Hopetoun in 1721
was that by the beginning of that year the Earl had eight children
and a wife who was again pregnant.[56]

The contract for work at Hopetoun which William Adam signed
in January, 1721, was for the building of an addition south of the
existing main block, entailing the replacement of the south-east
pavilion provided by Sir William Bruce in 1706 by a substantially
larger south-east wing containing a new family apartment providing for the Earl and Countess a bedchamber and two dressing-
rooms and two closets with servants' rooms still further to the
south. This new wing begins as a one-bay extension of Bruce's

main block before breaking forward in two steps, the second
projection being concave-sided. Adam's treatment of this addition
included widely spaced pilasters as at Bruce's Kinross House but
at Hopetoun the pilasters' Corinthian order and the treatment of
the addition's attic storey are taken from the engraving of Powis
House in London designed in 1714 and illustrated the next year
in the first volume of *Vitruvius Britannicus*, while the addition's
round-arched and key-blocked windows, perhaps derived from
the garden front of Vanbrugh's Castle Howard, and the concave
projection, are more decidely Baroque than anything in Bruce's
work.[57] There can be little doubt that the south-east wing begun
in 1721 was, from the start, intended to be balanced by a matching wing to the north and that some remodelling of Bruce's
main block, at least by the removal of his pediment and the addition of a balustraded attic like that on the new addition, was also
envisaged. What is uncertain is whether it was at first intended
to retain and complete Bruce's design of convex colonnades
joining the house to stable pavilions flanking the great forecourt.
If so, the build-up from the stables to the convex colonnades and
the concave-sided projection of the house's wings would have

Hopetoun House

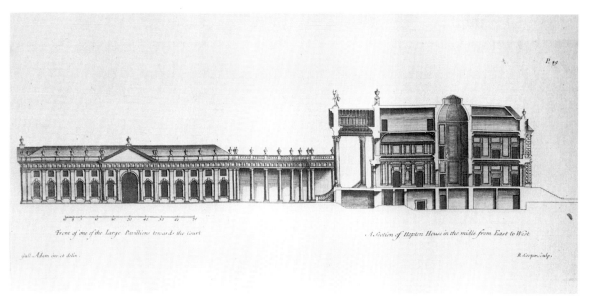

Front of one of the Large Pavillions towards the court   *A Section of Hopton House in the midle from East to West*

Jul.. Adam in. et delin.   *R. Cooper sculp.*

Hopetoun House.
William Adam's
design of 1726
(Vitruvius Scoticus)

given a dramatically Baroque swagger. Whatever the initial intention, by 1723, when John Macky visited, it had been decided to
broaden and enlarge the forecourt.[58] Work on the south-east addition was completed by 6 April, 1725, when it was measured by
William Adam, assisted by Lord Hopetoun's gardener Archibald
Shaw, 'at the sight of John Gordon and George Sherriff', and the
total bill of £8,661 0s. 10d. was paid on 15 May. In March, 1726,
after first getting an alternative estimate for the stonework from
Walter Morrice, the Earl of Hopetoun signed an agreement with
William Adam for building the south colonnade flanking the
forecourt, adding in a note that:

> My Lord is to give Mr. Adams over and above the said prices a com-
> plement of twelve pounds sterling, but Mr. Adams is to make my
> Lady a present of a marble table or marble chimney to the value
> of six pounds.[59]

This colonnade begun in 1726 was a concave quadrant, most
of the Doric columns probably reused from Bruce's convex
quadrant but with a new entablature to which Adam added a
triglyph frieze. The colonnade was intended to join the main
house to a long stable pavilion, its thirteen-bay front articulated
by Doric pilasters and with attached half-columns at the
pedimented three-bay centre. The result would have been Palladian of a bookish sort but only the colonnade was built as a result
of the 1726 agreement, and when the end pavilion was finally put

Hopetoun House.
Aerial view of
landscape layout

up more than ten years later it was to a different design.[60]

Hopetoun, like Floors, was intended to be the centre of a landscape which was designed by William Adam probably about the
time he was first employed at the house.[61] The layout may have
been partly decided by Bruce whose Baroque garden conventions
it generally follows with a formal parterre to the west of the house,
a great east avenue focused on the island of Inchgarvie, with North
Berwick Law beyond, and straight rides cutting through woodland.
After comparing the parterre favourably with that of Canons and
describing the view from the terrace to the north over and up and
down the Firth of Forth as 'the finest View I ever saw any where;
far beyond *Frescati*, near *Rome*, or St. *Michael del Bosco*, near
Bolognia, for Variety'. John Macky in 1723 added that:

There are also several Visto's from each of the many Walks that
run from this Parterre; some of them ending in a Parish Church,
some in an old Tower. And through the great Avenue fronting the

Palace, your View terminates on *North-Berwick Law*, near the
Bass, at Thirty Miles Distance, appearing like a Sugar-Loaf.[62]

Within two years of having begun work on the 'houses of state'
of Floors and Hopetoun William Adam was involved in the production of a house and landscape of comparatively diminutive size
but for a patron whose estimate of his own connoisseurship was
far from small. In 1722 Sir John Clerk inherited the estates of
Penicuik and Mavisbank from his father and decided to sell his own
small property of Cammo and build a 'small house' at Mavisbank,
a project formerly contemplated by his father who had gone so
far as to 'make several designs for this House with his own hands,
but at last thought himself too old to begin to build Houses.'[63] By
30 January, 1723, Clerk had consulted Adam and received from
him a design with an accompanying letter to explain:

> Im affraid by what I understand from the Directions ye name in
> yor Last, that ye'l think this I've sent too Large; But att the same
> ye'l see it a very small Box, and Genteell too . . . [64]

From the letter it is clear that the plan provided by Adam
included the main elements of his plan for Floors with both the
state apartment and the main family rooms on the ground floor
and, on the first floor, bedrooms 'with a Billiard Table Room Ser-
veing for ane Ante Chamber to the whole floor'. Above was to be
'a parapett wall in form of ane Attick', presumably a high attic of
the type so frequently illustrated in *Vitruvius Britannicus* and
used in the south-east addition to Hopetoun.[65] It was probably to
this design that Clerk referred when he wrote disparagingly:

> In the building of this House my Architect contended about
> making it a story higher, in which if I had complied, the fabrick
> wou'd have lookt like a Touer, and been quite spoiled . . . [66]

In sending his design William Adam seems to have had at least
a suspicion that Clerk would think it not good enough, for clearly
Clerk had suggested a design along other lines. Despite a sore
throat Adam was working on the design for an addition to
Newliston but promised that:

> so soon as its done I'le try my hand on something Like qt ye
> propose of a Cag th'o I cant say, the Dispositione will answer fully

so well as this Sent . . . and shall heartily Comply with any thing
of your oun thought, that may be judg'd Better then mine . . . [67]

The appearance of the proposed house was settled to Clerk's
satisfaction a few months later whereupon, according to Clerk,
work began at once:

> In May 1723 I not only finished my design for the House of
> Mavisbank, under the correction of Mr. Adams, a skilful Architect,
> but laid the foundation of the House . . . [68]

Responsibility for the design was firmly claimed by Clerk who
added that 'however the Architecture may please or displease, it
is oueing chiefly to my self!'[69]

Clerk's design for Mavisbank, produced under Adam's 'correc-
tion', was for a five-bay house of two tall storeys skied above a

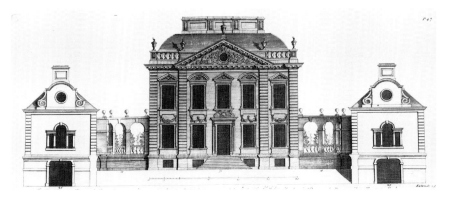

Mavisbank
(Vitruvius Scoticus)

Mavisbank.
Pediment

basement. The general conception seems to have been derived
from Colen Campbell's house according to a 'New Design of my
own Invention in the Style of *Inigo Jones*' published in the first
volume of *Vitruvius Britannicus* with a dedication to the Duke
of Argyll. Like the centrepiece of Campbell's house, Mavisbank is
of five bays with an urn-topped balustrade enclosing a convex-
sided piended platform roof. But Mavisbank's slightly projecting
pedimented three-bay centrepiece and pedimented first-floor
windows are probably taken from Jacob van Campen's Maurit-
shuis at The Hague and the carved swags and cartouches below
these windows owe much to engravings published by Vingboons.
The channelled strip pilasters emphasise the Dutch verticality.
Inside, the house was arranged quite differently from Adam's suggestions of January, 1723. On the ground floor were the family
rooms and entrance hall from one side of which rose a grand stair
to the first floor state apartment, a dog-leg sequence of dining-
room, drawing-room, bedchamber, closet and dressing-room, the
very rooms which Adam had stated 'shoud always be in the first
floor [i.e. ground floor] above the vaults'.[70] The plan must, on the
evidence of Clerk's poem 'The Country Seat', be ascribed to the
patron not the 'skilful Architect'. Although Clerk referred to
Mavisbank as a villa,[71] the house hardly conforms to his
recommendation:

> Not long suspended let your thoughts remain
> What form to choose, that always is the best
> Which the Pavilion of a Persian King
> In bulk and Beauty may resemble most.[72]

However, Mavisbank is much closer to his stipulation for the
Usefull House or 'House of Convenience'. Clerk laid down that:

> Its Front from Eighty to an Hundred feet
> May be extended with proportioned Breadth
> Which never under Forty Feet must fall . . .[73]

and, although Mavisbank's front is barely over fifty feet long, its
breadth is just over forty feet. Mavisbank does not conform to
Clerk's rule that the height should not exceed two-thirds of the
length, but its plan could be taken as the exemplar of what he was
to recommend only four years later:

By a large Open Stair or Portico
We may ascend from a neat spacious Court.
Here may a Loby or Salon be plac'd . . .

From this lobby a stair was to lead to the 'Chief Floor' containing:

with more capacious Rooms
All made to entertain our better Friends
A line from sixteen feet to twenty two
May measure out the Breadth of any Room.[74]

The rooms of Mavisbank's state apartment are all just 16 feet broad.

Disagreements between Clerk and Adam occurred during the construction of the house suggesting that Clerk had second thoughts about the details of his design. As early as August, 1723, the carver Isaac Silverstyne had been sent from Kirkcaldy to work on the swags and cartouches of the front,[75] but in October, 1724, after the roof had been put on, the detailed treatment of the pediment was in question, Adam telling Clerk:

As to the Pediement on the Fronts, affter considering all that matter fully, I am of oppinion that one window in the Midle of the Pediement will have the best Effect with a Large peice of Foliage on each Syde, & that all the Leaffs Flowers or Fruits be very Large on being farr from ye Eye . . .

Clerk's suggestions for a different treatment were politely but firmly squashed:

As to the removeing of the Coat of Arms from above the Door to the Pediement, Is what I doo not like So well, For one reason, I'm Very Sure that the Coat of Arms is So Small that it wou'd make no appearance att all att So great a distance, nor would it bear any proportione to the Massieness and Strength of any of the oy^r Sculpture that woud Join itt in the Pediement—Another is, that to fill up that Space where the Coat of arms is now with the Crest wou'd be too massie and Strong, and So outcharge the Cartooses or oy^r ornaments their . . . [76]

Adam won his point, Mavisbank's pediment being given a large bulls-eye window surrounded by deeply undercut foliage and the coat of arms being placed above the door. The next year's disagreement was about the flight of steps in front of the entrance. On this occasion Clerk prevailed, Adam conceding:

> As to the Stair I can easily yield that point, Tho' Your Lo[rdshi]p
> will See in Paladio's Architecture that Stairs are very offten the
> whole Length of the Front . . . [77]

At the same time as they were discussing the entrance steps Clerk
and Adam were considering the siting of the office pavilions each
side of the entrance court, Adam arguing that they should be as
far as possible from the main block, giving among other reasons
the inconvenience of 'Smoak by ye pavilions being too near the
House'[78] and urging unsuccessfully that they be:

> Litle, or at Least that they be Litle in appearance, For which I doo
> think the Octagon the best Form . . . [79]

The pavilions as built were rectangular and far from
inconspicuous, their fronts pierced by Venetian windows and
topped by scrolled chimney stacks. Linked to the house by tall
quadrants they made a composition of Baroque movement.

The landscape around Mavisbank was probably laid out by
Clerk by 1726 when he bought English elms and limes from
William Miller at Edinburgh. The court in front of the house was
treated as a parterre. Beyond, a *patte d'oie* of three broad avenues,
the ground between thickly planted, ran out to the country
beyond. South of the house was a wilderness in which were
placed inscribed pedestals and through which a winding path led
to two gardens, the one circular, the other rectangular.[80] Behind
the house was a mound preserved by the antiquarian Clerk who
had identified it as 'a Roman Station'.

By the summer of 1727 Clerk had:

> furnished up some Rooms at Mavisbank, wherefor I went and lived
> there with my Wife and part of my Family for the months of June
> and July when the Court of Exchequer was siting, and from thence
> roade every morning to Edin., which I found contributed greatly
> to my health.[81]

The great stair and first floor state apartment were still
unfinished. On 20 December, 1727, Adam assured Clerk that:

> As to yor Lo[rdshi]p[s]. Stair Caise and finishing any part of the
> Apartm[t]. above the Stairs in Stucco I am most heartily Satisfyd to
> do it in the best Manner and Your Lo[rdshi]p shall make the
> price . . .

At the same time he was suggesting that the balusters and hand-rail of the stair be of mahogany, although quick to deny that he was trying to offload the wood, 'Being my design was to use it where I was concernd my Self', and also suggesting that there be:

> a litle pillar at the Foot of the Stair, & one at every turn of the half pace & Flat above, with a litle Capitall at the top of each, which I observ'd commonly done & very handsome.[82]

By May of the following year the treatment of the stair hall seems to have been agreed but Adam who by then was employing two plasterers, one of them the stuccoist Samuel Calderwood, was having to juggle the claims of competing clients anxious to have their houses finished.[83] As he explained to Clerk,

> It gives me great uneasiness that I have not been able to get yo[r] Staircase finished ag[t]. the time yow fixt. I did speak with My Lord Sommerville, that he woud delay His Dining Room a Litle, Seeing the rest of the House would not be Soon finished—I am to speak to My Lord this day again about it, and will endeavour to get one of them for Yo[r]. Lo[rdshi]p and the other for Barron Dalrymple who is likeways very angry that his Stair Case is not finishd, I do declare I'd ra[yr] want my meat, then have the thought of dissobligeing my friends . . .[84]

Clerk's plan of Mavisbank was adapted by William Adam for two houses he designed in 1726. Craigdarroch in Dumfriesshire was built for Alexander Ferguson, a laird who had sat in Parliament as Member for the Dumfries burghs between 1715 and 1722.[85] Externally it is old-fashioned and unadventurous, the main block a piend-roofed box dressed up with a pedimented centre bay, joined by quadrants to simple pavilions.[86] Inside, however, the arrangement of rooms on the ground and first floors

Craigdarroch
(Vitruvius Scoticus)

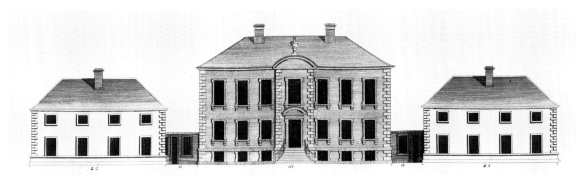

was virtually identical to Mavisbank, except that, as Craigdarroch is a little larger, Adam was able to provide additional bedrooms on the ground floor and, on the floor above, to place behind the grand stair a second apartment of bedchamber, dressing-room and closet but served by its own turnpike stair so that access to it was independent of the state apartment.

Somerville House (now The Drum) is much flashier. Adam's client, James, twelfth Lord Somerville, was the descendant of lairds too impoverished to think themselves fitted to claim the vacant Somerville peerage. When he himself was orphaned in 1710 at the age of twelve his income was only 4,000–5,000 merks a year from which he had to maintain his brothers and sisters. However, in 1722 he successfully laid claim to the peerage and, two years later, acquired as his wife Anne Baynton the only daughter of a Wiltshire landowner and widow of Edward Rolt *Somerville House* of Sacombe Park for whom James Gibbs had designed a *(now The Drum)* new house.[87] The design prepared by William Adam for Lord

Somerville House (now The Drum)

Somerville's mansion in 1726, seems to be related to a design which Gibbs was to publish as Plate 43 in *A Book of Architecture* in 1728, but treated with an undisciplined enthusiasm for the sculptural effects attainable by a skilled master mason.[88] The two-storey-and-basement main block is of only three bays with a pedimented centre and urn-surmounted balustrade but the front elevation's stonework is rusticated, providing a busy background for the windows' Gibbs surrounds and the first floor's blocked Ionic pilasters. Some recognition of Palladian precepts is shown by the pediments over the first floor *piano nobile*'s windows and the large Venetian window lighting the state drawing-room in the

Somerville House (now The Drum). State Dining Room

WILLIAM ADAM 1689–1748

centre with the owner's coat of arms placed, in accordance with Palladio and as Clerk would have liked, in the pediment above. Straight links, each with a roundheaded niche, its half-dome carved with a shell, flanked by windows in a heavily rusticated neo-Venetian arrangement, were designed to join to boldly advanced piend-roofed pavilions of which only the west (incorporating a fragment of an earlier house on the site) was built. Inside, the main block contains fewer but larger rooms than do either Mavisbank or Craigdarroch, everything apparently designed for show. On the left of the hall, its fireplace framed by Ionic columns and surmounted by a grandiose stucco trophy, is the family dining-room with Ionic columns appearing again at the fireplace and to carry the basket arches of the sideboard recess's screen. On the right of the hall were the family bedchamber with a dressing-room behind. At the back of the hall, on the main axis is the stair, a cantilevered timber oval lighted at the top through a Venetian window. From the stair's head is entered the state dining-room occupying the full thirty-six foot depth of the house, with another Venetian window in its east wall opposite the

Mellerstain. Design probably by William Adam, 1725

The North Front of Mallererstane House Toward the Court. Extends 110 feet.

fireplace whose overmantel contains a stucco relief of Neptune. In the centre of the coved ceiling is placed an octagonal relief of Jupiter and Juno. From the dining-room's south-west corner opens the state drawing-room in the centre of the front, beyond which lie the state bedchamber and dressing-room.

William Adam's predilection, of which he had informed Clerk in 1723, for a ground floor state apartment, found expression during the early 1720s in designs for a number of houses with an axial hall and saloon off which opened the state apartment to one side, the family apartment to the other. One of these schemes was produced in about 1725 for the Earl of Marchmont's brother-in-law George Baillie of Jerviswood for whom Adam built office pavilions at Mellerstain.[89] Apparently at the same time he produced plans and elevations for a new main block, externally of the Anglo-Dutch type popularised by Bruce and Smith twenty years before, the main fronts dignified by pedimented centre-pieces and dressed up with carved Gibbsian swags. On the entrance front, the ground floor *piano nobile*'s openings have Gibbsian surrounds and alternating segmental and triangular pediments. On the garden front's centrepiece the ground and first floor windows are round-arched and rusticated. Inside, was to be a T-plan hall composed of three twenty-foot cubes, its tail leading to the saloon off which opened on the left the state apartment of drawing-room, bedchamber and dressing-room and, on the right, the family apartment. Each side of the hall's tail was to be a round stair leading to an octagonal ante-chamber, perhaps an echo of Marly, above it. South of the ante-chamber the library occupied the space over the saloon.

At the same period William Adam produced a much grander scheme for rebuilding Newliston for his patron the Earl of Stair. Like Mellerstain it was to remain unexecuted. The design of the main front of Newliston was derived from Colen Campbell's executed scheme for Wanstead but with the portico covering three rather than five bays and consequently reduced from a two-storey to a single-storey height. The order also was changed from Corinthian to Ionic. Inside, the plan reproduced some of the main features of the Mellerstain scheme, with a T-plan hall opening into an axial saloon, twin stairs flanking the T's tail and with a library as the principal first-floor room, although at Newliston it is placed above the hall rather than the saloon.

Very probably the result of Stair's patronage was his brother's and brother-in-law's employment of William Adam. In 1724

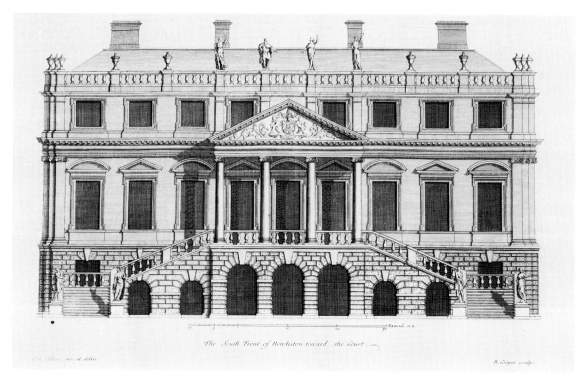

The South Front of Newliston toward the Court

Newliston. Design by
William Adam
(Vitruvius Scoticus)

Colonel James Campbell of Lawers whose sister Eleanor had
married Stair in 1708,[90] commissioned Adam to remodel and
extend Lawers House in Perthshire, the result unexciting with only
the pedimented centrepiece hinting at the intended showiness of
the first-floor saloon and drawing-room behind.[91] The next year
Adam began Belvidere (now Dalmahoy House) near Edinburgh
for Stair's younger brother George Dalrymple, one of Sir John
Clerk's colleagues on the Court of Exchequer. In the design the
influence of James Gibbs's executed scheme for Ditchley in
Oxfordshire was very strong. Like Ditchley Belvidere had a severe
main block with advanced ends but it is shorter and consequently
the centre bays do not project. Ditchley's high attic was omitted
and a balustraded parapet substituted, as was an imperial stair to
the entrance in place of Ditchley's straight flight.[92]

The most ambitious of William Adam's executed works of the
1720s was for another lawyer, Robert Dundas, who inherited the
Midlothian estate of Arniston from his father in 1726. Dundas was
described memorably, if not altogether reliably, by James Ramsay
of Ochtertyre as:

> all his life exceedingly fond of company, or, in other words, of his
> bottle, without which, in those days, there was little society.

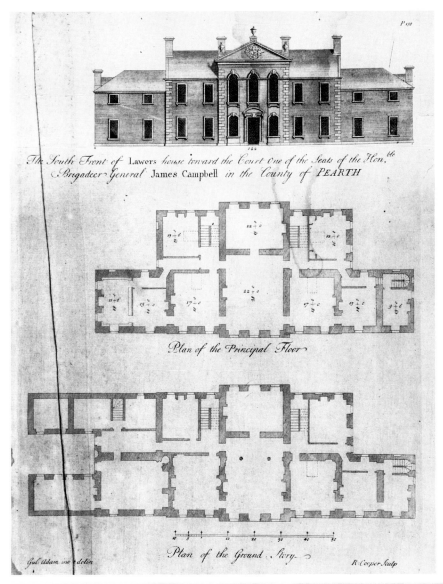

*Lawers House
(Vitruvius Scoticus)*

The South Front of Lawers house toward the Court One of the Seats of the Hon.ble Brigadeer General James Campbell in the County of PEARTH

Plan of the Principal Floor

Plan of the Ground Story

Gul. Adam inv. et delin.   R. Cooper Sculp

*Belvidere (now
Dalmahoy House)
(Vitruvius Scoticus)*

Generall Front of Belvidere toward the West the Seat of the Honourable George Dalrymple Esq.
one of the Barons of His Majesty's Exchequer

Besides frequent potations at his own house in Edinburgh after
business was over, he was often in the tavern . . . But at Arniston
for a number of years he kept what would now be called open
house, where friends and neighbours came uninvited and met
with cordial welcome . . . At the head of his own table he made
a joyous and respectable figure, none knowing better how to give
conversation an interesting turn; and whether it was grave or
lively, he took no more of it than was acceptable to his guests. In
truth, a great deal was to be learned from him over his cups, which
was not to be had from books or from other people.[93]

This genial, although sometimes irascible, lawyer, was also a

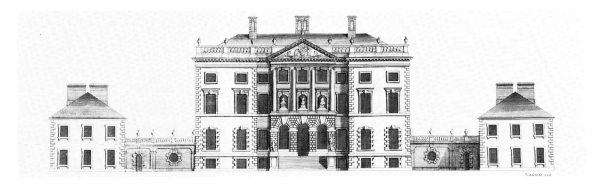

Arniston House
(Vitruvius Scoticus)

politician linked to the pro-Hanoverian but anti-Walpole faction
of the Duke of Roxburghe and the Earl of Stair. In 1726 he had
just been forced to resign as Lord Advocate but was still Dean of
the Faculty of Advocates and Member of Parliament for
Midlothian.[94]

The rebuilding of the mansion house of Arniston was to provide
a seat grander than Clerk's 'house of convenience and use' and
approaching in grandeur his 'house of state'. As his main source
for the front elevation William Adam seems to have taken James
Gibbs's design of 1720 for Down Hall in Essex. Like the intended
Down Hall, Arniston has a three-bay centrepiece with a temple
front raised above a rusticated ground floor pierced by round-
arched openings. The detailing of the windows of the outer bays
is also similar; corniced at the first floor, of horizontal proportion
on the floor above. But there are significant differences. Down
Hall was to have been of seven bays with a projecting centre, the
ground floor a loggia to carry the first floor's portico in front of
tall round-headed windows which are on the same plane as the
front wall of the rest of the walling. At Arniston, which is of nine
bays, the ends are advanced while the centrepiece projects only
far enough to allow the ground floor to carry attached columns
supporting the pediment. Between these columns are not single
tall first-floor windows but a two-tier arrangement of corniched
niches, intended to contain busts, and key-blocked rectangular
second floor windows. The Down Hall design has a horizontality
given it by the continuous rustication of the ground floor and the
treatment of the second floor as an attic above the main cornice.
Arniston, where the rustication is confined to the centrepiece
and the second floor is below the cornice, the pediment thus
rising against the balustraded parapet rather than in front of a
blind attic, is much more vertical, this quality heightened by Vanbrughian chimneys. The pomposity of Arniston's main block was

given a baroque monumentality by the balustraded screen walls panelled with basket-arched recesses in which are set rusticated octagonal openings, linking to the office pavilions enclosing the *cour d'honneur* in front. As at Somerville House Adam marked the presence of a state apartment on a side elevation of Arniston by giving the first floor's state dining and drawing rooms' west windows alternating segmental and triangular pediments with lugged panels above. However, this apartment's continuation along the garden front on the south is not acknowledged, that elevation left starkly severe except for the Vanbrughian blocked columns of the door from the ground floor Oak Parlour in the centre.[95]

In his planning of Arniston's interior Adam combined the ground-floor hall and saloon axis of his Mellerstain and Newliston designs with a first-floor state apartment such as was provided at Mavisbank, Craigdarroch and Somerville House. The hall is of baroque magnificence, quite contrary to Sir John Clerk's precept that the hall in a 'house of convenience and use' should not be inordinately large, rising through two storeys. Its central compartment is of two bays by three with fluted Corinthian pilasters supporting the coved ceiling cut into by groin vaults. In each bay are two tiers of round-headed arches, the lower extravagantly key-blocked, opening on three sides into aisles with first floor galleries. In the south wall, the two side arches contain

Arniston House. Hall

chimneypieces, a scaled-down version of what Vanbrugh had produced at Castle Howard. The general conception of the hall may
owe something to the stairhall at Beningborough in Yorkshire, but
as likely a source is the Cube Room at Sudbrook House in Surrey
which James Gibbs had designed for that Scottish potentate the
Duke of Argyll. The lavish stucco work was not executed until the
1730s and, although Adam doubtless intended suitably grandiloquent decoration, the detail was probably left indeterminate
when the house was begun. On the main axis a short corridor led
between the oval secondary stair and the front of the state stair
to the Oak Room, the principal ground-floor room in the centre
of the south front. Along the east and west sides of this floor were
placed the family's parlours, bedchambers and closets. The state
stair was designed to lead to the hall's west gallery from whose
north end a door opened into the state dining-room occupying
the northern two-thirds of the west side. From this the proces-
sional route led to the state drawing room in the house's south-
west corner and then along the south front to the state bedchamber, dressing-room and closet. Three secondary bedchambers and closets were placed along the east side of this floor.
On the second floor the space above the hall was taken up a cove-
ceilinged library, its bookcases framed by Ionic pilasters.

Not surprisingly with a house of such a size and with a client
whose political career had had only limited success and hence

Arniston House.
Library

limited financial rewards, it was decided to build initially only the eastern two-thirds, leaving the west part containing the state apartment to follow. Such a decision may have been taken partly because Robert Dundas was simultaneously engaged in the layout of the surrounding landscape, again using Adam as his designer. Here the baroque conventions of formal axiality were both followed and half-mischievously misapplied while the use of natural elements as a formal focus, which had been made much of earlier by Sir William Bruce at his own houses of Balcaskie and Kinross, was further developed. The great avenue from the entrance front was focused on the volcanic crag of Arthur's Seat to the north. South of the house the avenue's axial line was continued into the parterre and to the cascade beyond. The approach from Gorebridge was along an east avenue merging into a sanded *allée*, the avenue's line marked each side of the house by hollies. West of the house but off the axis of the east avenue, was a wilderness planted with larch and evergreens, its paths forming, as in the wilderness at Hopetoun, a twelve-point *étoile*. East of the house the wilderness was balanced by the kitchen garden and orchard.[96]

William Adam's patrons used their influence to try to get him government posts and contracts. In 1723 Parliament was considering a Bill to extend the provisions of an Act of 1717 enabling the burgh of Edinburgh to levy a duty on all ale produced in the town, the proceeds to be spent on public works in the city. Adam lobbied his clients for some additional clause to be inserted in the Bill, getting the clause drafted by the Marquess of Annandale who sent it to Lord Hopetoun in London:

> That incase it was past the House of Commons, My Lord Hoptoun might Lay itt befor ye Lords himself . . . [97]

Hopetoun also received a letter concerning the matter from Sir John Clerk but replied apologetically:

> I am heartily sorey your letter came not sooner, the town of Edinbrugh's Bill was past both houses tuo dayes befor I receved it, I wish it had been sooner thought of for I realy believe the thing might have been done. I do assure you I should have been very willing to have done Mr: Adam's all the service that was in my pouer . . . [98]

Unfortunately these patrons did not record the nature of the suggested additional clause, but among the Act's main provisions were ones for 'building a proper Hall, or other Conveniencies, for accommodating the Court of Justiciary' and for building a repository for legal records.[99] It stated that the Town Council was to carry out these works:

> and particularly for Building proper Repositories for keeping the Publick Records; and that they shall, and they are hereby directed and required to advise with, and imploy Men of the Best Skill and Knowledge in such Matters . . . [100]

Perhaps the extra clause was to name William Adam as the architect to be employed.

Four years later, in 1727, the Earl of Stair approached Sir Robert Walpole to have Adam appointed Surveyor of the King's Works in Scotland at a salary of £100. This came to nothing, apparently because of the death of George I later in the year.[101] However, although the King's death prevented Adam acquiring the title, he received most of the accompanying salary, Sir John Anstruther of Anstruther, Member of Parliament for Fife and Master of Work to the Crown in Scotland, devising a method by which he could maintain his own position as a dispenser of patronage while giving satisfaction to Adam's influential patrons. As he explained to Sir John Clerk at the end of 1727:

> I afterwards thought it might be ane easy matter for Mr Adams who had a great many freinds, to procure Mr Murreys post of clerk to the works with a hundered pounds of sallery, I therfore mentioned it to him with this condition that he was to give Mr Murray 30 pounds a year out of it, which Mr Adams very readily came into, as this is Mr Murrays present sallery I thought it could be no prejudice to him If Mr Adams got it in this shape, but rather strengthened his interest by my joining those who had made application in favour of Mr Adam . . . [102]

The next year Adam was duly appointed Clerk and Storekeeper of the King's Works in Scotland and two years later Mason to the Board of Ordnance in North Britain.[103]

It was probably partly in connection with this search for a government post that William Adam visited London at this time, but a second reason for the journey was to find an engraver to prepare plates of his drawings for publication. The trip was being

planned as early as May, 1726, when Adam informed Sir John
Clerk:

> I write My Lord Stair Lately, and told him that if it was not possible
> for me to get up this Summer that if I Liv'd shoud certainly goe
> with his Lo[rdhsi]p the end of this year. & that in the meantime
> I'm getting Doubles of all my Draughts to carry with me in order
> to put them in the Engravers hands—This puts me in mind to
> desire the favour of the Draught of Mavisbanck with the offices,
> for I want a Clean Coppy from it.[104]

The journey was at last undertaken in March, 1727, Adam joining
up at Stamford with Sir John Clerk who, recently having become
the first Scot to be elected a Fellow of the Society of Antiquaries,
was travelling to London at the invitation of his antiquarian
acquaintances, the Earls of Hertford and Pembroke, Roger Gale
and Dr William Stukeley. From Stamford, Adam and Clerk visited
Burghley House but were refused admittance as the family was in
mourning. They were more fortunate at Wimpole Hall near Cambridge which James Gibbs had recently enlarged for the Earl of
Oxford, although Clerk noted disparagingly of the gardens:

> . . . no water or water-works here, only some fish-ponds . . .

On arrival at London they took lodgings in Suffolk Street which
had been booked for them by Clerk's cousin the painter William
Aikman.[105] For the next month and a half Clerk was entertained
by English antiquarians, met Lord Burlington, and paid his
respects to English and Scottish nobles noting complacently of
the latter that:

> My Country Men at London were all very civil to me, particularly
> the Dukes of Hamiltone and Argyle, Roxburgh, and Montrose; the
> Earls of Illay, Aberdeen, and others.[106]

While Clerk viewed the sights of London and its suburbs and
made an expedition to Wiltshire to see Wilton (whose contents
he apparently found more agreeable than its architecture),
Salisbury Cathedral and Stonehenge,[107] Adam was probably in
the company of his patron Lord Stair, making political and
governmental contacts, and taking preliminary steps for the
engraving of his drawings. At the same time he sat for his portrait
to William Aikman, as did Stair.[108]

Adam seems to have remained in London for some time after Clerk's departure on 16 May and, although he had certainly returned to Scotland by September, as late as December 1727 he was making excuses for having had:

> to run about my litle affairs, which requir'd to be put into Some order, which my Stay in England requird after I got home . . . [109]

On getting back to Scotland Adam began to collect subscriptions for his book of engravings, the subscribers receiving receipt forms which seem to have been engraved and printed in London. On 17 September 1727, the Earl of Rothes was issued with receipt number 28 recording his payment of three guineas as the first of two instalments due for two copies. Two months later Lord Dun became the seventy-second subscriber and by March 1728, one hundred and thirty-five receipts had been issued. The receipts call the book only 'My Designs for Buildings &c. in 150 Plates' but in 1733 the English antiquary James West noted that:

> Mr Adams, the architect, is about publishing and engraving all the fine buildings in Scotland to make a *Vitruvius Scoticus* . . . [110]

The title with its obvious allusion to Campbell's *Vitruvius Britannicus* was probably intended from the start. Certainly Campbell's formula of publishing the works of earlier architects as a prelude to his own designs seems to have been adopted. But, possibly because of the relative scarcity of subscribers,[111] or perhaps because of the slowness of the engraver or even Adam's own diffidence, the plates were not to be printed until about the time of his death and not published for more than another sixty years.[112]

William Adam's work in the 1720s was not confined to architecture. He engaged in a variety of entrepreneurial activities, mostly but not all connected with the building trade. When Sir John Clerk in 1728 visited the Linktown brickworks, he wrote in his diary:

> This I found as expensive a piece of work as the nature of it required and I could not enough admire the enterprising nature of the proprietor who had at that time under his own care near to twenty general projects—Barley Mills, Timber Mills, Coal Works, Salt Pans, Marble Works, Highways, Farms, houses of his own a-building and houses belonging to others not a few.[113]

The year 1728 can be seen as marking Scotland's acceptance of William Adam as 'the universal architect' of the country. On 21 February the Edinburgh Town Council voted to admit Adam as a burgess and guild brother of the City *gratis* for services rendered to the town,[114] and it was probably later in the same year that he moved his family from Gladney House at Linktown to Edinburgh.[115] By then he had two sons, John who had been born in 1721, and Robert, born at Gladney on 3 July, 1728, a third son William having died in infancy.[116] Perhaps the move from Linktown was made easier by the death, also in 1728, of Adam's father-in-law and partner William Robertson.[117] Henceforth Edinburgh was the base from which William Adam undertook his multitude of activities.

Chapter 7

HOUSING THE GREAT
AND GOOD

In 1743 William Adam stated that he:

> for these many years past had devoted himself to the Service of
> most of the Nobility and Gentry in this Country [Scotland] who
> being possest of plentifull Fortunes Liberally educated and
> endowed with a genius for Architecture did incline to erect
> Palaces or houses Suitable to their Rank & fortune in the
> world . . . [1]

As an account of his career between moving his family to Edinburgh and his death in 1748 this was not a boast so much as a
statement. Not surprisingly many of his clients had links with
others. Adam worked not only for the first Earl of Hopetoun but
also for two of his sons-in-law, the Earl of Findlater and James
Watson of Saughton. He was architect to that powerful pair of
brothers, the second Duke of Argyll and the Earl of Ilay, as also
to their nephew the third Earl of Bute, and supplied the Duke's
former *aide-de-camp*, Colonel James Stuart, with a design for
Torrance House. As well as working for the second Earl of Stair
and his brother George Dalrymple of Dalmahoy, Adam designed
Balgregan for their niece's husband John McDowall. The second
Earl of Marchmont, for whom he had produced the over-expensive
scheme for remodelling Redbraes Castle, was the uncle of Helen
Home whose husband Andrew Wauchope of Niddrie Marischal
also received from William Adam a design too costly to build.
Adam's extensive work at Yester for the fourth Marquess of
Tweeddale may have had something to do with his earlier com-
mission to design a house of the Marquess's uncle, Lord William
Hay. Another of Lord Tweeddale's uncles, the fourth Duke of
Hamilton, was likewise a patron, as was Hamilton's first cousin
Lord Daer. Sir John Anstruther of Anstruther was first cousin to
Colonel Philip Anstruther of Airdrie, and Robert Dundas of
Arniston was first cousin to Charles Erskine of Tinwald.
   Some of these clients, whether through choice or political

misfortune, lived on their estates and engaged in agricultural improvement. Several, such as Colonel Philip Anstruther of Airdrie, Lord Daer, Lord William Hay and Colonel Stuart of Torrance, were soldiers. Lords Dun, Milton and Minto were all judges of the Court of Session and Charles Erskine of Tinwald, later himself a judge, was successively Solicitor General and Lord Advocate of Scotland. Some held government posts and enjoyed their income. Lord Belhaven was General of the Mint and a member of the Board of Manufactures, Sir John Anstruther of Anstruther a Member of Parliament and Master of Work to the Crown in Scotland. The third Earl of Bute was a Lord of Police; so too was the Earl of Findlater who also held the office of Vice-Admiral of Scotland. Adam's grandest clients, although they did not necessarily indulge in the largest building projects, had accumulated a quantity of government posts. The second Duke of Argyll had been High Commissioner to the last Scottish Parliament. Later he became Commander-in-Chief of the Forces in Scotland, Master-General of the Ordnance, High Steward of the Household, and finally Commander-in-Chief of the British Forces. His politically more astute brother Archibald, Earl of Ilay, held government office for over fifty years, for most of the time as the 'Scottish minister' in London, being appointed Lord Justice General of Scotland in 1710, Keeper of the Privy Seal in 1725, and Keeper of the Great Seal in 1733. Government generosity extended to those who supported the Hanoverian dynasty only in a private capacity like Henrietta, Duchess of Gordon, who brought up her children as Protestants instead of in the Catholic faith of her husband, and was rewarded with an annual pension of £1,000.

The designs produced by Adam for these clients pick up themes from his earlier houses. The combination of an axial hall and saloon with a ground floor state apartment appears at House of Dun, Haddo House, Mount Stuart and Gartmore, and in the unexecuted schemes for Elie House, Torrance House, Kenmure Castle, Fasque Castle and Cally. The diminutive box of Hamilton Hall had a state apartment arranged as a circuit like those of Mavisbank and Craigdarroch but here it was on the ground floor. The first-floor state apartment recommended by Sir John Clerk for the 'house of convenience and use' appeared at Balgregan House, Cumbernauld House, Duff House and in the designs for Prestonhall, Saughton House and Lonmay House. Only in the design for the Duke of Montrose's Buchanan House was the state apartment omitted altogether.

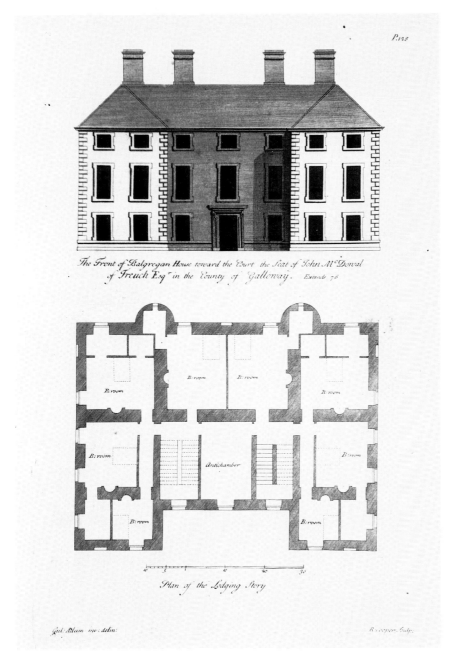

Balgregan House
(Vitruvius Scoticus)

The exteriors were varied. A few had an almost rustic plainness. The design for Fasque, perhaps because it was for the extension and remodelling of an existing house and perhaps also because the client Sir Alexander Ramsay of Balmain was a baronet of only limited wealth and political ambition, was old-fashioned. It looked back to the formula devised by John Mylne and Sir

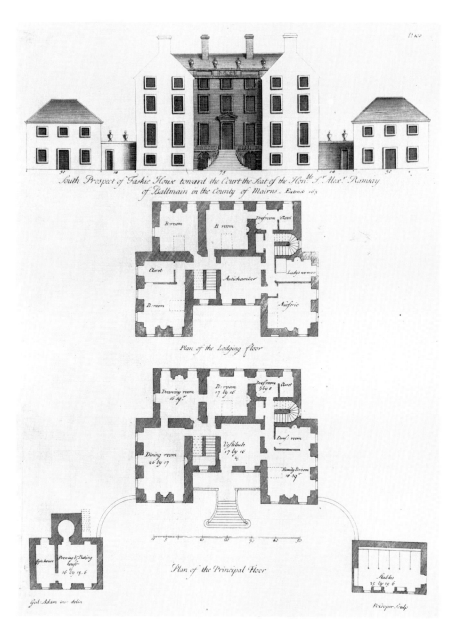

William Bruce in the 1660s and 1670s of a U-plan wrapped round
a parapeted centre. Balgregan House of about 1730, designed for
another owner of limited ambition, was very simply treated with
piend-roofed wings and a lugged and corniced doorpiece of a type
which might have looked fashionable fifty years earlier. This was
one of a small number of William Adam's houses not to have the
entrance floor raised above a basement. Another example would
have been the unexecuted Lonmay House in Aberdeenshire, a
severely plain piend-roofed block with flanking pavilions

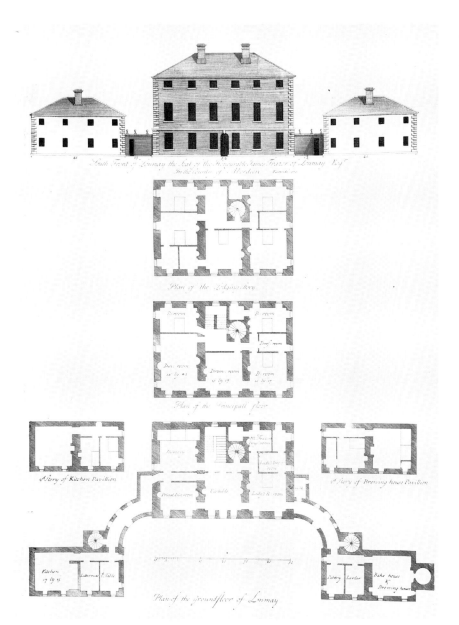

designed for a younger son of Lord Saltoun who was not one of Scotland's richer peers. The greater wealth and large government pension enjoyed by the Duchess of Gordon were expressed by Adam's design of about 1740 for Prestonhall, whose thirteen-bay main block, its entrance again firmly on the ground, would have been a severe barrack relieved only by the central niches intended for sculpture. The architectural display was confined to the pavilions flanking the *cour d'honneur*, their pedimented centrepieces containing boldly rusticated Venetian windows.

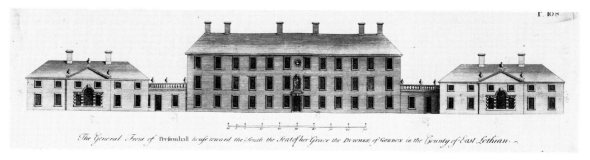

The General Front of Prestonhall house toward the South the Seat of her Grace the Dutchess of Gordon in the County of East Lothian.

Prestonhall. William Adam's design (Vitruvius Scoticus)

The influence of Colen Campbell and James Gibbs in pushing English architects to design understated Palladian country houses affected a number of William Adam's designs, apparently produced for clients who eschewed any hint of flashiness. The main block of Haddo House, built in 1732–5 for the second Earl of Aberdeen, is a restrained box with tightly grouped windows in the pedimented centrepiece where the entrance to the *piano nobile* is approached by a semicircular perron.[2] Arcaded single-storey quadrants (since heightened) curved forward to solid piend-roofed pavilions. Very similar was the design of Tinwald House in Dumfriesshire built in 1738 for the Lord Advocate Charles

Buchanan House. William Adam's design (Vitruvius Scoticus)

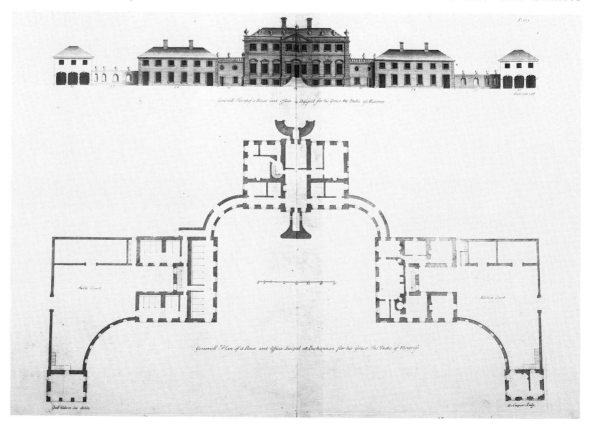

Erskine but at Tinwald the basement has channelled rustication
(omitted in execution) and at the centre of each side elevation
is a semi-octagonal projection containing closets. Even more
austere, lacking even a parapet, was the main block of Mount
Stuart built by the third Earl of Bute with Gibbsian rustication at
the door and windows giving it a military severity. The suavest of
these neo-Palladian designs was produced for Buchanan House
in 1741, the main block being given angle pilasters at the ends
and centrepiece and the ground floor windows crowned with
alternating segmental and triangular pediments. The design for
Buchanan House shows a vastly extended *cour d'honneur* with
short two-storey concave quadrants joining the main block to the
stable and kitchen ranges which are in turn joined by single-
storey quadrants (masking the service courts behind) to end
pavilions whose outer walls are 150 feet from the corners of the
main block.

Very assertive centrepieces were produced in 1731 at Cumbernauld House for the Earl of Wigtown and in about 1740 at Gartmore
for the Perthshire laird Nicol Graham. At both houses the centre's
walling was carried up to support a pediment skied above the

Cumbernauld House
(Vitruvius Scoticus)

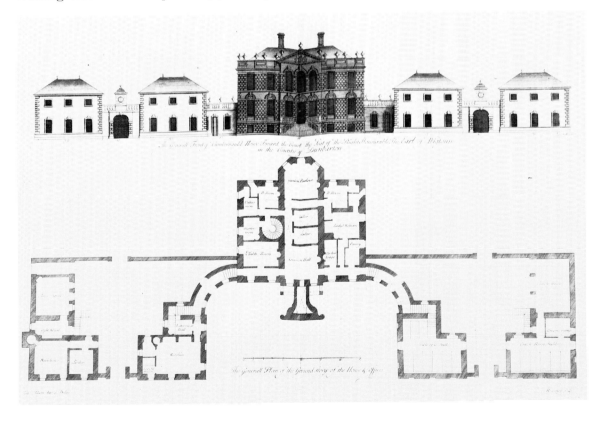

parapet. The centrepiece's vertical emphasis was heightened at Cumbernauld by roundheaded first floor windows, at Gartmore by an etiolated Venetian door under a Venetian window. A similar Venetian door in a pedimented centre was the main focus of Adam's unexecuted design for Cally House but its impact would have been overpowered by the proposed Imperial stair, its form probably taken from Campbell's Wanstead House engravings. A more ambitious design with a pedimented centrepiece pushed up above a balustrade was that for Torrance House in Lanarkshire where Adam adapted 'A Draught of a House made for a Gentleman

Gartmore House
(Vitruvius Scoticus)

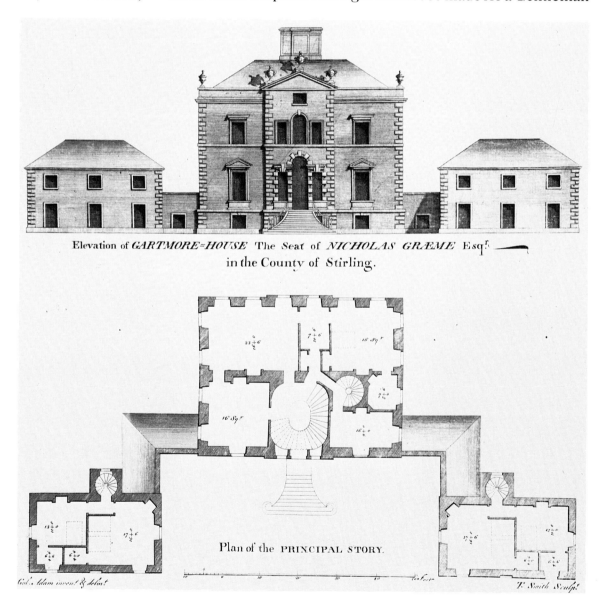

Elevation of *GARTMORE=HOUSE* The Seat of *NICHOLAS GRÆME* Esq.
in the County of Stirling.

Plan of the PRINCIPAL STORY.

in 1720' published in James Gibbs's *A Book of Architecture*. Like this prototype the Torrance design had superimposed Doric and Ionic pilaster orders with a tripartite door under a Venetian window, but in Gibbs's design the Ionic order is properly confined to the window while at Torrance it would have risen above to support the pediment. For Gibbs the orders were frames for the openings, for Adam they formed the wall itself.

William Adam's not infrequent delight in an exuberant combination of architectural details was amply demonstrated by his design of about 1740 for Kenmure Castle. The U-plan entrance front was given a pedimented centrepiece, the tympanum intended to be filled with carved heraldry. The fronts of the wings were pierced by large Venetian windows. On the garden front where the ground fell steeply the basement became a full two storeys, above which the *piano nobile*'s pedimented centre windows were surmounted by circular niches designed to contain busts, an external revelation of the presence of the two-storey saloon within, just as had been done on the front of Arniston to mark the presence of a two-storey hall. The same device was proposed again in Adam's design for a remodelling of Elie House for Sir John Anstruther of Anstruther. Elie's new west front would have been generally of the Haddo and Tinwald type but with a giant Corinthian order applied to the centrepiece whose openings would have been round-arched and key-blocked and surmounted by the niches, once more disclosing a two-storey room behind. At Elie, like

Torrance House. William Adam's design (Vitruvius Scoticus)

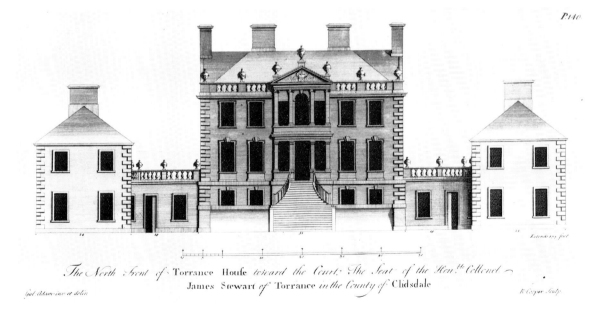

P.140

The North Front of Torrance House *toward the Court; The Seat of the Hon.ble Collonel James Stewart of* Torrance *in the County of* Clidsdale

Gul: Adam inv: et delin *R: Cooper Sculp:*

One of the End Fronts of Castle Kenmore

Extends 74 feet

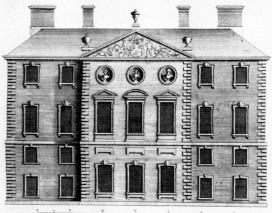

West Front of Castle Kenmore faceing the Loch

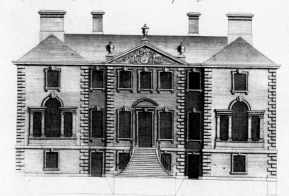

Extends 80 feet

The East Front of Castle Kenmore toward the Court

Wil: Adam invt et delin

R: Cooper Culp

Kenmure Castle.
William Adam's
design (Vitruvius
Scoticus)

Hopetoun, the quadrants to the service pavilions would have been colonnades (Ionic rather than Doric) with passages behind.

In his design and construction of these houses Adam had sometimes to deal with patrons who sought advice or reassurance from such *cognoscenti* as Sir John Clerk of Penicuik and Lord Hopetoun who had made the Grand Tour in 1724–7.[3] At Haddo the Earl of Aberdeen consulted Clerk, sending him thanks in December 1731:

> for the many good advices your letter contains, which were not only extrely kind, but very seasonable to me; who am so litle knowen and unexperienced in Building . . .

and especially for recommending the mason John Baxter 'who is so knowing and diligent in his business'.[4] Baxter had been Clerk's main contractor at Mavisbank but had been supplanted for at least some of the work by William Adam, perhaps one reason why he quibbled about the design for Haddo.[5] As the Earl explained to Clerk:

He [Baxter] is under some difficulties with respect of some things

Haddo House
(Vitruvius Scoticus)

Elie House. William Adam's design
(Vitruvius Scoticus)

The General Front of Haddo House designed for the Rt Honble the Earl of Aberdeen in the County of Aberdeen

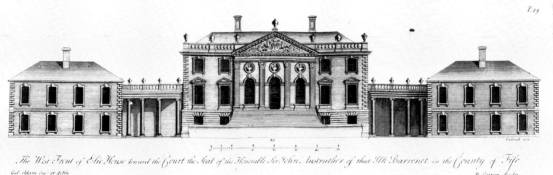

The West Front of Elie House toward the Court the Seat of the Honorable Sir John Anstruther of that Ilk Baronet in the County of Fife

in M[r] Adams Draught which I intreat your Lo[rdshi]p will have the
goodness to allowe him to lay before yow, that I may have the
honour of your lo[rdshi]ps approbation, in such alterations as shall
appear necessary to your lo[rdshi]p I shall soon write to M[r] Adams
that he may waite of your lo[rdshi]p att any tyme when yow have
leisure and then your lo[rdshi]p will please hear M[r] Baxter and
him, and then I beg your lo[rdshi]p will please determine what
yow think best.[6]

Despite this show of diffidence Lord Aberdeen did not prove an
easy client, Baxter 'finding' in 1732 'the noball Earle whom I
serve very absolout in his oun opinion in building'.[7] Perhaps
Adam got on better with him than did Baxter with whom Adam
was clearly at odds. In July, 1733, Baxter's problems with the

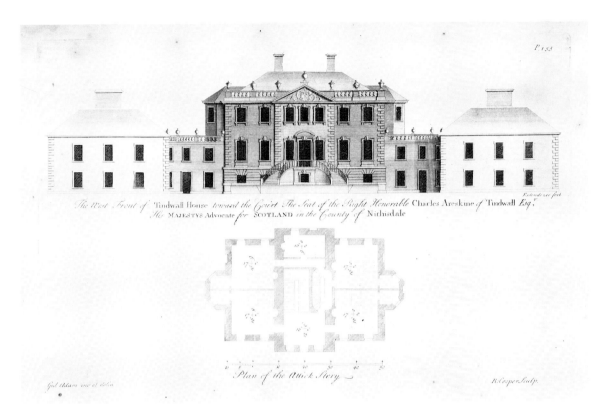

The West Front of Tindwall House toward the Court The Seat of the Right Honorable Charles Areskine of Tindwall Esq.
Her MAJESTYS Advocate for SCOTLAND in the County of Nithsdale

Plan of the Attick Story

client had lessened and he was able to report triumphantly to Clerk:

Tinwald House
(Vitruvius Scoticus)

> My lord is better to worke to this year then he was the last and I have don all thats in my poure to pleas him he seis planly nou that the storys Mr Adams advancd to him is false and without foundation for the house Stands weill without Crack or flor or the least simptem of a sitte in any pairt of the whoal so Mr Adams is disapointed who thought to have turnd me of with disgrace and got the work all in his oun hand . . . [8]

When his new house of Tinwald was being built Charles Erskine received a note from Sir John Clerk to say that he might be going to Dumfriesshire and that 'if I go I'll pay a visite to your Masons if you have any Commands for them'.[9] However, the next day the workmen were visited by William Adam accompanied by Lord Hope who wrote an account of the expedition to Erskine:

> Mr Adam after having made me wait several days for him at Leadhills at last join'd me, & we went to Drumfries together on Fryday last & early next morning to Tindwall, where we spent a

good Part of the Day in viewing what is allready done & concerting
the necessary measures for finishing the Work, & then I left him,
he being to stay some Days to give directions to the different
Workmen.[10]

Two days later, after his return to Hopetoun, Lord Hope wrote
again to Erskine to reassure him that 'You will be here time
enough to settle the form of the Stair' and to say that he and Adam
had given thought to the layout of the landscape at Tinwald.[11]

Lord Hope's Grand Tour may have been influential in deciding
the design of the later stages of William Adam's work on remodelling and extending his father's seat of Hopetoun. The heads of an
agreement were drawn up on 7 February 1728. These provided
for the building of 'the new designed north addition', identical in
every respect to Adam's earlier south extension except for being
two feet longer. It was agreed also to enlarge the state apartment's
dining-room to the north by twelve feet, this room becoming the
first room of a new state apartment in the addition, replacing
Bruce's state apartment in the main block. Bruce's entrance front
was now also to be refaced and pilasters placed between the
windows. Of Bruce's design for this front, only the windows
remained and even those of the centrepiece became rectangular
although Adam's design engraved for *Vitruvius Scoticus* had
shown them as still round-arched. That engraving showed also a
deeply projecting Corinthian portico and a curved perron,
neither of which was to be executed.

The work covered by the agreement of 1728 was completed in
1731 and four years later the north colonnade was begun,
matching Adam's existing south colonnade. On the colonnade's
completion in 1736 work was started on the extension of both
colonnades from eight to eleven columns' length and on the erection of the pavilions at the east end of the *cour d'honneur*. An
unexecuted design for these was engraved for *Vitruvius
Scoticus*, perhaps in about 1730, showing that they were then
intended each to contain identically planned stable and coach
house accommodation. In the executed scheme begun in 1736
the north pavilion was given over to stabling, with careful differ-
entiation between hunters, coach-horses and work-horses, while
the south pavilion was to house a billiard room, study, library and
laboratory. The pavilions' external design was altered significantly. The engraved scheme had shown them with fronts of thirteen bays to the court and of five bays to the east, the three centre

Hopetoun House.
Centrepiece of main
front

Hopetoun House.
North stable
pavilion

bays of each advanced under a broad pediment carried by
attached Doric columns, the outer bays articulated by Doric
pilasters. In the executed scheme the pavilions are each of seven
bays by seven with only the centre bays pedimented, the pilasters
are paired and repeat the colonnades' Tuscan order. On the roof
of each pavilion is a Gibbsian cupola, a feature not shown in the
earlier design whose rather nervous elegance has been sacrificed
to provide a soberly well-dressed prelude to the swagger of the
house's main block.

Some panelling and marble chimneypieces and pedestals were
installed in the house between 1739 and 1744 but the interior of
Adam's north extension seems to have been left unfinished.
Plates engraved for *Vitruvius Scoticus* in about 1730 show that
Adam had produced designs for remodelling the interior of
Bruce's main block. Two of them show the hall pushed up to a

Hopetoun House.
William Adam's
design for the
Saloon
(Vitruvius Scoticus)

height of two storeys, its coved ceiling enriched with stucco work rising above pilastered and panelled walls. A third engraving shows Bruce's garden parlour in the centre of the west front also heightened to two storeys with an upper tier of oval windows under the ceiling's cove. The plan and section engraved for *Vitruvius Scoticus* both show the removal of Bruce's central stair to make a tribune rising the full height of the house. That these schemes were not executed is not altogether surprising. They would have entailed the removal of a number of existing bedrooms and made circulation on the first floor more difficult. Perhaps more seriously for a Scottish nobleman of the early eighteenth century, they would have produced a hierarchical con- flict between the axial progression of hall, tribune and saloon or garden parlour, and the right-handed progression through the intended state apartment to the north.

The first Earl of Hopetoun died in 1742, the same year as the pavilions were completed. Little work was done at Hopetoun during the remaining six years of William Adam's life but, in May 1745, it was calculated that he was still owed about £1,000 and, when the accounts were finalised the next year, the total cost of the north colonnade, the extension of the south colonnade, and the pavilions was stated to have been £4,443, Adam stating his profit to have been about £300. On the memorandum recording this the second Earl of Hopetoun noted 'I gave his son John a present of 50 guineas . . .'[12]

William Adam's client at House of Dun near Montrose was David Erskine, an Angus laird and lawyer, who had studied at the universities of St Andrews and Paris, represented his county in the Scottish Parliament of 1690–6 and later been noted as an opponent of the Act of Union. Despite this act of political opposi- tion he was, in 1710, appointed a Lord of Session with the title of Lord Dun and in 1714 given also the lucrative post of a Lord of Justiciary.[13] It was recalled of him that:

> As he spared no pains in discharging the duties of his laborious office, so he was accounted a man of honour and integrity, both on and off the bench. His piety and zeal for religion were conspicuous, even in times when all men prided themselves upon being decent in these matters. The pedantry of his talk and the starchiness of his manners made him the subject of ridicule among people who had neither his worth nor innocence of heart and life. He was likewise overrun with prejudice, which sometimes warps the judgement of able, well-intentioned men; but for that, one would be at a loss to

account for his Toryism which approached very near to
Jacobitism . . . In his notions of Church government he was
decidedly Episcopal both in public and private. It did not serve to
set off what he said to greater advantage, that he spake a language
peculiar to himself, which he called English.[14]

In 1723 Lord Dun had obtained a design for a new house on
his estate of Dun from Alexander McGill, apparently a smaller
version of Sir William Bruce's design for Craigiehall. McGill's
design was sent to Dun's kinsman the Earl of Mar, then a Jacobite
exile in Paris, who condemned it:

*David Erskine, Lord
Dun, by William
Aikman*

There wou'd Scarce be a tolerable good room in that whole house
& it would be fitter for a Gingate (as its named here) for a Burges
near to a great town, than for a Gentlemans seat in the Country,
wch. is to go from father to Son, as is hoped for many generations
where tho the house may not be large nor great appartments in
it, yet ought to have one or two handsome & tolerable large rooms
for the Master to entertain his friends upon occasion & where
Some Copels of young folks may dance when they have a mind
to divert themselves at Peace Yull & high times . . . [15]

Not content with dismissing McGill's design, Mar sent one of his
own for a tall square house of three storeys with a basement, attic,
an *entresol* over half the ground floor, and a belvedere roof.
Although he described it as 'only a Pavilion' Mar was at pains to
provide five ground floor rooms of which three were to rise through
the *entresol*, these being intended:

for parad & a principal Stranger when there comes any such . . . [16]

Of the two lower ground-floor rooms, one was the hall and the
other was to be for Lord Dun, whose bedchamber was placed
above it in the *entresol*, opening off the private dining-room.[17]
The corners of the main block were to be linked by screen walls
to four pavilions defining corners of the forecourt, gardens and
parterre.[18] Mar's three-bay fronts, all with segmental pedimented
centrepieces with giant Ionic pilasters framing a two-storey
round-arched recess, were derived from the triumphal arch
treated with Baroque gusto. The design may have been too daring,
or Lord Dun's resources too limited, for he did nothing for a
further eight years. Then, in 1731, he received a second design
from Lord Mar, possibly sent because of Dun having commissioned a scheme from William Adam.[19]

This first design by William Adam for House of Dun showed an
internal plan very close to what was to be executed later. The
elevations, however, were markedly different. These were for a
simple piend-roofed box, the entrance front's one-bay centrepiece having Doric columns *in antis* supporting the segmental
pedimented upper floor. The elevation to the garden would have
had a three-bay pedimented centre with tall rusticated round-
arched ground floor openings.[20]

Adam's second and executed design was, as he noted on the
engraving in *Vitruvius Scoticus*, 'more ornamented than the

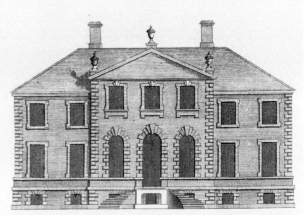

The Garden Front of Dun house
as first Design'd Extends 78 Feet

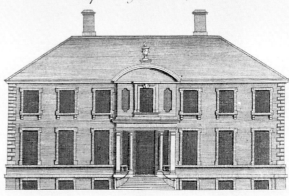

The Court Front of Dun House toward the North

A The Laigh Hall
B The privat Kitchin & Scallerie
                    under y' Stair
C The Nurserie
D Closets & Back Stair to the Ladys
                    room at foot
E Cellars
F Second Table room
G Litle bed room and Closets
H Woman House
I Larder
K Latter meat Hall
L Pantry
M Milk room
N Porter lodge under y' Stair

A Plan of the Ground Floor

gul: Adam inv: et delin:

*House of Dun.
William Adam's first
design* (Vitruvius
Scoticus)

former'.[21] The entrance front's three centre bays were treated as an Ionic pilastered triumphal arch, the door and window above set well back within a broad round-headed arch, the stair windows each side contained in narrow overarches, again round-headed. The round arch theme was continued at the outer bays' ground floor windows. The roof was masked by an urn-topped parapet which became a balustrade over the centrepiece. On the garden front the changes from Adam's first design were fewer but just as telling in raising the social status and architectural quality of the house. At the outer bays the ground floor windows were corniced instead of having lugged architraves. At the centrepiece a balustrade was substituted for the pediment and the ground-floor openings tied together by being placed in rusticated stonework which rose to the springing of their round-headed arches, a device illustrated by James Gibbs in his engraving of 'a House design'd for a Person of Quality in *Somersetshire*'.[22] The house's resulting appearance lacked the exuberance of Mar's schemes, having a more sober though still baroque magnificence. A curiosity is that the deep recess on the entrance front has little effect since it faces north and receives direct sunlight for only a few days each year. Mar however had justified such a recess on the north front as providing shelter from the wind for the rooms behind and making the house warmer.[23]

Adam's plan is beatifully clear. On the main axis lie the hall and saloon. Down the east side is the state apartment opening from the saloon with the standard progression of drawing-room,

House of Dun

*House of Dun.
Saloon*

*House of Dun. State
Drawing-room*

bedchamber, closet and dressing-room. On the west side are the parlour and family bedroom with, to north and south, dressing-rooms, a closet and the charter room. A staircase each side of the hall led to the first floor where a library in the centre of the garden front above the saloon provides another grand family room among the surrounding bedrooms and closets.

At House of Dun William Adam's rôle as a co-ordinator and supplier of craftsmen for internal finishing was strongly evident. The hall and saloon's stucco decoration was executed by Joseph Enzer who worked for Adam also at Arniston and Yester.[24] The hall's round-headed and pilastered panels and overarches he filled with baskets and drapes of fruit and foliage. The saloon was made a grandiloquent stucco exhibition of Jacobite iconography with high relief figures of Neptune and Mars, the gods of the sea and war who were to bring the rightful king from over the sea and place him on his throne, facing each other from above the fireplaces at each end. In the cove above Neptune, bathing *putti* are encircled by the depiction of a stag hunt. Above Mars, a goddess sits in the midst of a huge military trophy with shackled captives at her feet. On the long south wall's cove are emblems of music and agriculture, on the north wall heraldry and portrait busts. Fruit-filled vases stand over the doors to the family apartment, military trophies at the entry to the state apartment. Enzer's work extended into the parlour and the state drawing-room where his foliage is placed above a two-tier marble chimneypiece of the type which Adam had recommended for Mavisbank, with:

> Mirrour Glass to Stand in a Large Fraime of Marble of the Same kind of work with the Chimney it Self, & finished att top with a marble Astragall . . . [25]

Work at Yester for the fourth Marquess of Tweeddale occupied William Adam from 1729 almost until his death. As early as March, 1726, he had mentioned to Sir John Clerk that he had been to Yester 'to doo some things there for the Marquiss',[26] and in July of that year Lord Tweeddale paid 6d. postage on receipt of a letter 'from Mr Adam Architect'.[27] However, it was not for another three years that any major work was undertaken.

When the Marquess had succeeded his father in 1715 he had inherited debts as well as estates, being informed by his mother:

... ye circumstances of ye family are very loe at present above 30000 lib in debt so yt ye anuel rents & keeping of our crydett & paying y^m. punctually must take some considerable manadgment ... [28]

By 1729 matters had improved, the Marquess now being an Extraordinary Lord of Session and one of the Scottish peers elected to sit in the British House of Lords, and Lord Tweeddale was able to contemplate finishing the unfloored shell of the main block of Yester House which had been built for his father by James Smith.

John, fourth Marquess of Tweeddale, by William Aikman

Smith's plan of the interior had provided for an axial hall and saloon, both rising through two storeys, with a ground-floor state apartment on one side. Although such a plan probably had some appeal to William Adam, its grandeur fitted badly with comfort, the family apartment on the ground floor being cramped and circulation on the first floor awkward. Whether the initiative for a radical alteration of the plan came from Adam or his client is unclear but by 1729 Adam had prepared plans for the insertion of a floor across the upper level of the projected hall and saloon, the saloon's lower part being made a garden parlour in the same position as those at Hopetoun and Arniston. Adam proposed that most of the ground floor be given over to family rooms. On the left of the hall he placed a drawing room off which opened a suite of dressing-room, family bedchamber and closet. On the right of the hall were to be the private dining-room, a closet, Lord Tweeddale's dressing room, and the charter room. Each side of the garden parlour was to be an apartment of bedchamber, dressing-room and closet, presumably for guests. Adam placed the state apartment on the first floor with a saloon or 'Great Dinning Room' above the hall, the state drawing-

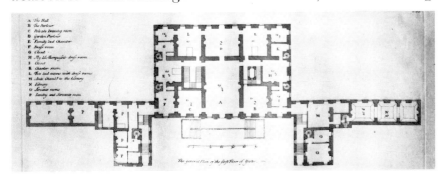

Yester House. Plan of ground floor (Vitruvius Scoticus)

Yester House. North front (Vitruvius Scoticus)

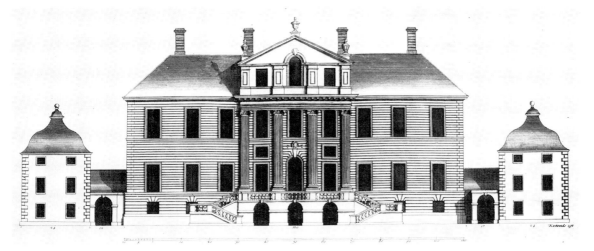

room above the garden parlour and, on each side, an apartment
of bedchamber, dressing-room and closet. The saloon and drawing
room were each to be twenty-nine feet high necessitating the
raising of an attic above the three centre bays of the entrance and
garden fronts. This plan was evidently not quite what Lord Tweeddale had first intended, for Adam felt it necessary to state that:

> In the Drawings I receavd from Your Lo[rdshi]p, that which I
> designe Dinning Room & Drawing room is Turnd into a Gallery
> which no doubt wou'd make one exceeding fine room; But in my
> oppinion breaks the State Appartment, & which will certainly
> make one among the first in this Country.[29]

The new pedimented attics above the saloon and drawing-
room Adam suggested should be carried on an attached order
applied to the centre bays of each front. Writing about the
drawings he had sent to Lord Tweeddale for approval he
explained:

> I have rais'd 4 Three Quarter Columes on the Front with Cappitals
> and a full Intabliture after the Corinthian order This I doo think
> is much wanting, to take of the Plainness of the Front And one can
> more propperly raise the Attick above it . . . I perswade myself your
> Lo[rdshi]p will see that this woud add a great Grace to the Front—
> And I doo think is much wanted—Your Lo[rdshi]p may Likeways
> repeat the same on the Garden Front, or with Pillasters in place
> of ¾ Collumes. It may doo plain; But as the whole of this ornament
> woud amount to no great Sum, I doo think your Lo[rdshi]p woud
> think the Charge well bestow'd in the Event.[30]

Lord Tweeddale was evidently not as easily persuaded as Adam
had hoped of the desirability of these alterations, in the event
agreeing only to the application of a relatively cheap Ionic order
of pilasters to the entrance front. He seems to have discussed the
matter with Sir John Clerk who now appears as someone familiar
with building costs as well as taste. In October, 1729, the Marquess told Clerk:

> After you went from Yester I had a good deal of discourse with Mr
> Adams and was at last prevailed upon to agree to four pilasters
> after the Ionic order to be added with an attick to the Court front;
> I have in a manner agreed with him as you'll see by a copy of the
> minute inclosed . . . as you had a great hand in perswading me to

finish itt as it is now designed I have sent you a copy of the minute
thatt you may peruse itt before we sign the contract and shall hope
you'll be so good as to acquaint me of any clauses you may think
necessary to be added particularly to secure me yt he may finish
itt sufficiently, I have likeways sent you a copy of the estimate he
formerly gave mee without pilasters, yt you may have some notion
whether whatt I have agreed to pay him now with the addition of
Pilasters be too much . . . [31]

The contract for the addition of the attics and pilasters, together
with alteration of the roof from an M-roof ('which Lodges a Great
quantity of Snow in the winter Season to the Great prejudice of
the said roof') to a platform, was signed on 20 December, 1729.[32]
The price was £1,100 out of which Adam had to pay for wood and
lead, Lord Tweeddale providing other materials.[33]

The Marquess did not prove the easiest of clients. By April,
1730, he was fussing about the spacing of the pilasters. Since the
windows of the nine-bay front were grouped 3/3/3, it was impossible both to place all the pilasters in the centre of the walling
between windows and to have them at equal distances from each
other. Lord Tweeddale's suggestion that they be placed in the
centre of the walling between windows was met by Adam with
a recitation of architectural textbook knowledge:

> The disposition concerted and which is according to rule is this,
> that whatever the distance is betwixt each of the two midle
> pilasters and the windows on both sides of each pillaster marked
> A the same must be the distance, betwixt the inside of each of the
> outtermost Pillasters and the windows next to the Pillasters
> marked B, This makes all Regullar within the 4 Pillasters Cald in
> Architecture a Tetrastyle, and what falls without this Tetrastyle
> does not Concern us, as to the strick rules of Architecture I mean
> the ornamentall part . . . This is a Coledge on Architecture which
> I'm sorry yor Lo[rdshi]p does not like better.[34]

Perhaps overawed, the Marquess seems to have conceded the
point.

In 1734 the Marquess failed to be re-elected as a representative
peer in the British Parliament and William Adam's work at Yester
during the next eight years, when Lord Tweeddale was in the
political wilderness, was confined to a fairly leisurely fitting up of
the interior. At the end of 1731 he had been about to produce drawings for the hall and garden parlour but a memorandum of 1734

listing work to be undertaken then suggests that little had yet
been done and the house's main block was still unoccupied.[35]
Among the improvements suggested by Adam in 1734 was the
installation of:

> a water Closet with a marble stooll its thought will be most pro-
> perly situate under the litle back stair that is to be placed betwixt
> what is now my Lord Marquiss's bed Chamber [in the west
> pavilion] (afterward to be turned into a biliard Room) & the
> Library, This water Closet will be more retired here then in any
> other place of the ground Story.[36]

At the same time the coving of the ceiling over the great stair was
to be made, Adam providing a mould for its cornice, capitals for
the garden parlour's panelling were to be carved in Adam's
workshop, and a bell-cord from Lady Tweeddale's bedroom in the
east pavilion to the woman house installed.[37]

By 1737 the main block's ground floor seems to have been
habitable and Adam submitted his account for providing marble
chimneypieces. That supplied for the garden parlour was excep-
tionally expensive at £83 9s. 9d., not surprisingly since its frieze
and pediment were carved with 'Scrolls & flowers of the Car-
touses in Statuary marble'.[38] Work was in progress on stucco
decoration, Joseph Enzer occupying a room sparsely furnished
with a 'Tent Bed wt A Canvas Bottom', a 'new firr Table wt a
Drawer' and a pewter chamberpot,[39] and assisted by his apprentices Philip Robertson and Francis Nicols.[40] For his work Enzer
was paid an annual salary of £55.[41] On the stairhall's coved ceiling
Enzer placed rococo cartouches in the corners and, on the long
sides, reliefs of jolly *putti* and a staghunt like that at House of Dun.
The hall's plasterwork is more formal but again hinting at the
rococo. He was working in the garden parlour when he died, this
news being given to the Marquess in a letter of 5 July 1743, from
William Adam:

> Poor Joseph Enzer died last week; Among the last things he
> did was altering a Trophy he had done over the pediment of
> the Chimneypeice in the Garden parlour. I complain'd of it to
> him & indeed he has put a much better in its place, A Vase with
> some mosaick work. He has filled up the pannal of that Chimney
> where Your Lo[rdshi]p intended a picture, in Basso Relievo which
> is very neatly execute, & I dare say Your Lo[rdshi]p will be as well

satisfied with it as with any picture that could have been put
there.[42]

With the fall of Walpole in 1742 the Marquess of Tweeddale's
political career flourished. He was again elected a representative
peer and was appointed Secretary of State for Scotland. This position kept him largely in London but the income enabled him to

*Yester House.
Stairhall*

make further alterations to the entrance front by removing the
earthen ramp provided by Smith and erecting a formal stair in its
place. For this William Adam produced the design of an Imperial
stair but this was found too large and too fussily detailed by his
client who wrote from London in March, 1743:

> I have considered your last plan for this Stair, and am still of
> opinion, as I always was, that it is too large and extensive for the
> House, besides you have added some further Ornaments to it, such
> as your Niches which I dont like, since I desire it might be done
> plain without any Ornaments. I had a few Minutes Discourse with
> my Lord Pembroke, who entirely agreed with me in opinion and
> thought it would be better to have the Stair contracted; that it
> should continue in the same Shape but extend no farther than the
> side of the Window next to the Door, and have but one Arch under
> it instead of three. I have sent you down two old plans by which
> and by what I have formerly talkt with you on the Subject, I think
> you may be able to comprehend my Meaning; and therefore I
> desire you would immediatly on receipt of this, send me up a Draft
> of the Stair agreeable thereto that I may give orders that it may
> be set about immediatlye . . . [43]

Possibly this dropping of the name of Lord Pembroke, the owner
of Wilton, former patron of Colen Campbell and himself credited
as the architect (in association with Roger Morris) of the

Palladian Marble Hill House, caused William Adam to concede
the argument, though still protesting in favour of his design:

> That by keeping of the Stair near to the Front wall of the house
> the Windows on each side the Door of the Low hall were lighted
> thro' the Arcade below, And the four Pilasters stood up on the flatt
> of the Stair above which according to my notion of these things
> had a good effect.[44]

He duly prepared drawings based closely on the designs sent him
by Lord Tweeddale although his accompanying memorandum
makes it clear that he regretted not being allowed a continuous
horizontal balustrade to serve visually as a base for the pilasters
of the centrepiece:

> Tho' the pedestals of the two extream Pilasters on the Front of the
> house in both these designs are a little hurtfull to my eye; But this
> cannot be remedied as the Stair is shorten'd . . . [45]

He also pointed out that by following the designs sent him the
stair would project deeply into the forecourt 'which I am unwill-
ing should appear less than it is already.'[46] This brought a riposte
from Lord Tweeddale that those designs had not been intended
to be copied exactly but to serve:

> only as a sort of Aids to explain what I wanted & to show you in
> what taste & manner I inclined that the Front Stair should be
> shortened, and nothing more . . . [47]

The design of the stair finally agreed, it was built in 1744–5
although Lord Tweeddale may have had doubts about his
aesthetic and financial wisdom when in August, 1744, he received
a letter from his factor Thomas Hay:

> I dined at Yester last Thursday . . . I see the Great Stair at Yester
> going up I have no Skill & cannot Judge what effect it will have
> till it is further advanced but it seems bulky & I was surprised
> when Lord George [Hay] hinted to me that it might cost near
> £1200 st. A great house is a great drain . . . [48]

Completion of the front stair and Lord Tweeddale's ready
acceptance of the design for the simple flight of steps on the

garden front did not end Adam's problems with this powerful and opinionated client.[49] Lord Tweeddale now had doubts about the effect of the rectangular niches which Adam had placed in the entrance front's centrepiece to mark the height of the hall behind and was considering either filling them with low reliefs or building them up altogether. To the first suggestion Adam responded that:

> nothing could be rais'd there that would have a propper effect as it is far from the eye, & would look flatt as the Coat of Arms [over the door] betwixt the two are much rais'd.[50]

As to the niches being built up he argued that 'it would occasion too much dead wall at that place.'[51] Instead, he repeated the suggestion he had first made in 1734,[52] that they be filled with busts, although:

> What these figures are to be, I leave Your Lo[rdshi]p to judge, whether a Caesar & an Alexander or any others that may be more agreeable; And if they are in Lead I beleive will be cheapest, & laste time out of mind, considering they will be lyable to no accident.[53]

The solution of practical problems was a necessary part of William Adam's working life. At Yester his addition of an attic to the centre of the front in 1730 caused rainwater to collect at the junctions of the attic with the main roof. In 1745, Adam, without hinting that the problem was in any way his own fault, proposed:

> to place a rain water pipe on the outside of each of the extream pilasters on the north front, for conveying down the rain water that comes from the Leads. For as it is now not confin'd, it comes down in great quantitys in time of great rains & discolours the front wall of the house, which is hurtfull to the eye, & will in time do prejudice to some parts of the new Stair next to the house.[54]

James, fifth Duke of Hamilton, was one of the grandest of Scottish nobles of the early eighteenth century, descended from the Earl of Arran who had been heir to the Scottish throne and Regent during the minority of Mary, Queen of Scots, as also from the first Duke of Hamilton who had led a Scottish army against Cromwell in 1648. The Duke's estates included the island of Arran, rich farmland around Hamilton in Lanarkshire, and extensive coal mines in West Lothian where his burgh of Bo'ness was the entrepôt for trade between the firths of Forth and Clyde. Like his father whom he had succeeded in 1712 at the age of nine, the fifth Duke was suspected of holding Jacobite sympathies and

James, fifth Duke of Hamilton, by William Aikman

rumoured to have been made a Knight of the Thistle and of the
Garter by the Old Pretender. However, by 1726 he was at least
publicly reconciled to the Hanoverian dynasty, receiving the
Garter from George I in that year and being appointed a Lord of
the Bedchamber to George II in 1727, a post from which he
resigned six years later as a result of his opposition to the government of Sir Robert Walpole.[55]

Between 1727 and 1742 the Duke employed William Adam on
'making surveys & plans &ca at Hamilton' at a fee of 30 guineas
a year.[56] Hamilton Palace itself had been designed by James
Smith in 1693,[57] but was only half-built when John Macky visited
in about 1723:

> THE Palace is designed to be a Roman H. but the Two Wings to
> the Front are only finished, those to the Garden are left till the
> Duke is of Age. The Body of the Front is very handsome, being
> adorned with Pillars and Pilasters of the Corinthian Order; but it
> is not near Eighty Foot Broad, while the Wings are One Hundred
> and Fifty Long. This I thought very preposterous, and makes it
> look like Greenwich Hospital; but when the other Part of the
> House is finished, it will not appear so.[58]

For the completion of this house Adam proposed the curtailment
of the long south wings, their thickening by the addition of cor-
ridors along their outer sides and the addition of lateral exten-
sions at their ends. On the unfinished north side of the main

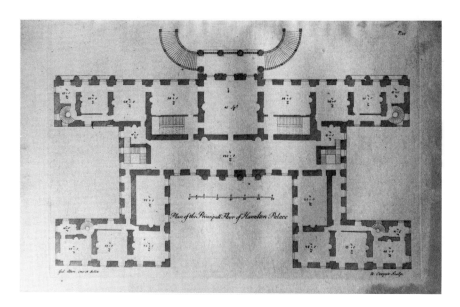

Hamilton Palace.
William Adam's
proposed plan
(Vitruvius Scoticus)

block he designed not matching wings as Smith had intended, but the conversion of the main block into a double-pile by the building of a longer north range. This range's elevation was derived from the engraving of 'a large House for a Gentleman in the County of York' published as plate 41 in Gibbs's *A Book of Architecture*, although at Hamilton the basement was not to project as a terrace and the ends were given greater emphasis with round-arched windows placed between attached Corinthian columns. The curved perron to the Corinthian portico was taken from another of Gibbs's designs, that for Milton House.[59] In the event none of this seems to have been carried out, a north range not being added until the early nineteenth century.

Near the Palace was the parish church which Adam rebuilt in 1733. The plan was fashionably progressive, a Greek cross whose arms project from a circular centre, perhaps directly inspired by Gibbs's first design for St Martin-in-the-Fields although Renaissance precedent for round churches was not hard to find. One limb of the cross housed the Duke of Hamilton's retiring room serving his pew in the gallery. The opposite arm contained the minister's vestry above an arcaded porch and was surmounted by a stolid cupolaed steeple sitting above the pediment.

Hamilton Palace. William Adam's designs (Vitruvius Scoticus)

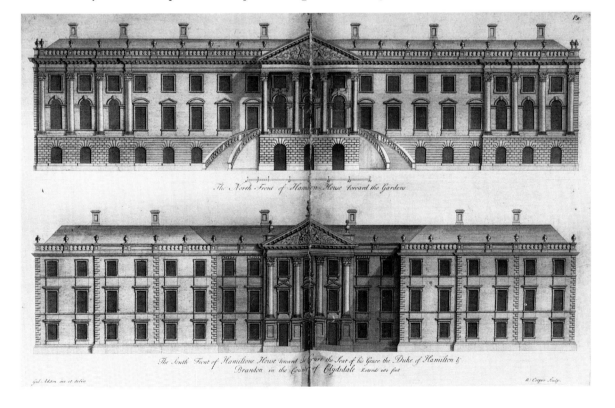

The landscape around the Palace had been laid out before
Adam began work there, Macky being able to describe:

> a great Park of Six or Seven Miles in Circumference, Walled round,
> and a lesser Park behind the Gardens, both well Wooded and
> Watered; the great Park having a River running through its Middle,
> and extreamly well stock'd with Deer.[60]

Its principal feature south of the palace was a straight avenue, the
lines of trees running uphill from the house's wings for a mile to
end on the edge of a ravine cut by the river Avon across which
lay the ruins of the Hamiltons' medieval stronghold of Cadzow
Castle. As a terminal feature to this avenue Adam designed an
'eyecatcher' containing dog kennels and a banqueting hall, this
'Dogg Kennell' as it is called on the *Vitruvius Scoticus* engraving

*Hamilton Parish
Church*

Chatelherault
(Vitruvius Scoticus)

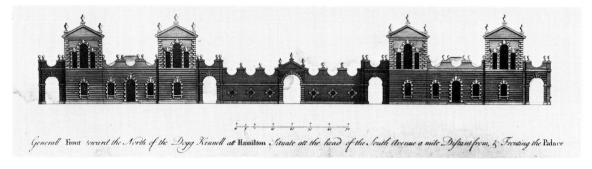

Generall Front toward the North of the Dogg Kennell att Hamilton Situate att the head of the South Avenue a mile Distant from, & Fronting the Palace

being formally known as Chatelherault in memory of the Duke's ancestor the Earl of Arran having been created duc de Chatelherault by Henri II in 1549.[61] Chatelherault is a 290-foot-long stretch of garden wall with pavilions breaking boldly forward, at each end the centre pierced by a pedimented gateway. The general concept is that of a French *hôtel* but the front of The Queen's College, Oxford, under construction at the same time may have been a particular influence. But at Chatelherault each pavilion is composed of two two-storey pedimented towers of Wilton or Houghton type flanking a single-storey three-bay centre block across which is carried the channelled rustication of the towers' ground floor, a design which may be derived from Inigo Jones's elevation for the Charing Cross front of Whitehall Palace. At these centre blocks of the pavilions and at the screen wall between the parapets are scooped up to carry stone balls. The elements are generally Palladian but handled with a baroque gusto which makes it regrettable that there is no record of the comments of Lord Burlington to whom the Duke intended to send a copy of the drawings in 1733.[62] However, Charles Bridgeman, designer of the formal Baroque landscapes of Stowe and Blenheim, on being shown the scheme, confessed:

> he was realy surprised to see it and did not think there was any body in that part of the world could draw so well and likewayes thought the building magnificent & what would cost one immence sume of monney.[63]

Preliminary work on building Chatelherault began in 1731,[64] and the exterior must have been largely complete by April, 1740, when the Duke urged Adam to come:

> from the infected City of Ed^n to the wholesome Air of your own Child the Kennell, and revell in the delights of yr owne production . . .[65]

However, the stucco decoration of the west pavilion housing the banqueting hall and rooms for the Duke was not begun until 1742 when the plasterer Thomas Clayton arrived.[66] On the banqueting hall's walls he placed emblems of music and hunting, its ceiling's cove he embellished with foliage twining round figures and the flat was given an arcadian relief. In the west tower's upper room, probably the Duke's closet, a relief of Diana resting fills the centre

of the ceiling. On the walls, swag-topped cartouches enclose stucco portraits, the decoration combining to produce an appropriately ducal lavishness of display.

Clayton had been first recorded in connection with William Adam in 1740 when he executed the ceiling of the state drawing-room at Somerville House.[67] From there he had moved to work on the apartment at Holyroodhouse occupied by the Duke of Hamilton as hereditary Keeper of the Palace, a refitting under the supervision of Adam who complained that he would:

> rather undertake to build a house where I can furnish the materials myself, than have to do with so many different folk who furnish different hands to so small a job . . . [68]

The work included the provision of marble chimneypieces, stucco work and panelling in which were set landscapes by the Edinburgh painter James Norie.[69] For the state bed the upholsterer David Shaw had 'promised a scratch of the newest

fashion in beds' but Adam insisted on a design 'agreeable to one
lately came from London for the Duchess of Gordon', with
damask hangings and a valance of 'water Harraton'.[70]

Adam's most difficult client was William Duff who had succeeded to the Perthshire estate of Braco on the death of a cousin
in 1719.[71] In 1722 he inherited his father's Banffshire estates
worth the huge sum of £6,500 a year.[72] According to his brother-
in-law William Baird, Duff:

got a very compleat education, and was a better scholar than most gentlemen commonly are, who have not been bred to any of the learned Professions. For he was master of the Latin, French and Italian languages, with some tincture of the Mathematics, and was very well acquainted with ancient and modern history.[73]

In 1727 Duff was elected Member of Parliament for Banffshire,[74] and three years later employed Adam:

to make out severall plans of houses for him . . . And for that end [Adam] made severall Journeys to Banffshire where part of his

William, Lord Braco,
by William Mosman

Estate lyes and visited the grounds and situation for a new house
as well as several plans for repairing and augmenting a house he
had in or near the Town of Banff . . . [75]

Nothing more, however, seems to have been done until 1734
when Duff decided not to stand for re-election to Parliament:

and being now resolved to Settle at home and his family pretty
numerous and yearly growing he also resolved for his Amusement
and better Accommodation to make Considerable alterations and
additions to his principall Mansion house near to the Town of
Banff . . . [76]

Accordingly, he employed Adam to produce plans for these alterations but in May, 1735, just before his elevation to the peerage as
Lord Braco, Duff:

had the favour of Seing at his house near Banff ane honourable
person of great Judgement and taste in Architecture, as well as
other more usefull things And after Showing and relateing to him
what he was about and viewing the Neighbouring or Adjacent
grounds higher up along the Same river Deveron the petitioner
[Duff] was advised that a certain place Somewhat more distant
from the Burrough of Banff, and building a new house there would
be preferable to the proposed design of repairing or adding to the
old house And the petitioner [Duff] at first was Somewhat loath
to embark himself in Such a great design But having attended his
honourable Counciller at Aberdeen And from thence to the house
of his friend Mr Duff of Premnay, he was there by their Joint Advice
Determined and from thence writt by express to Mr Adams to
repair to Perth against the twentieth of May and there Settle the
first draught of a plan and to bring it North to Banff. All which
being done and the Iron Struck while it was hot, the foundation
Stone of the new house was laid on the Eleventh of June one Thousand Seven hundred and therty five about a Month after the first
proposall of Such design.[77]

This rapid course of events meant that, when the house was
begun in June, 1735, the design had not been finalised or, at least,
was open to reconsideration. In October Lord Braco, as Duff now
was, approved Adam's plans for the basement and ground floor.[78]

At the same time and apparently at Braco's instigation, Adam produced a design omitting the attic which his client found:

> to Answer your own Satisfaction and my Intention for you have indeed Clypt the Attick Story and yet with the Turrets upon each Corner to go up to the roof of the house, you have preserved the height and beauty of the house and front . . . [79]

However, Braco expressed concern 'that the pavilions be not enlarged by this Alteration', a point to which he returned in March 1736, when he complained that 'the pavilions are much larger than I proposed'.[80] In May 1737, he changed his mind and agreed to the reintroduction of an attic storey:

> After I think back and forward on it I believe I'll not get over the Attick Story, because the want of it would Spoill the Looks of Such a Monstrous house and indeed I wish you and the house had been at the D-- before it had been begun . . . [81]

For Duff house, as Lord Braco named his new seat, Adam produced a design of a tall nine- by seven-bay house of two storeys and an attic above a fully exposed basement. As at Floors there was a tower at each corner but although Houghton was again the

Duff House

inspiration for these, at Duff it was not the Houghton towers as
designed by Colen Campbell but as executed by James Gibbs
with domed tops replacing the originally intended pediments.
Adam emphasised their verticality by superimposing a giant
order of Corinthian pilasters and a second order at the tall attic.
The house's centrepiece is a Corinthian pilastered temple front
with round-arched openings and a pediment rising against the
attic's panelled masonry much as he had proposed at Hopetoun.
In front he placed a horseshoe-shaped perron. The design's movement and modelling are unquestionably Baroque, the effect
heightened by the deeply undercut stone swags on the towers and
heraldry in the pediment. Adam intended this main block to be
joined by concave Ionic colonnaded quadrants to two-storey
pavilions, their roofs' cupolas and their fronts' coupled pilasters
again reminiscent of Hopetoun but with Gibbsian Venetian
windows as the central features. One pavilion was designed to
contain kitchen accommodation, the other a seventy-five foot
long library, its dimensions stated by Lord Braco to be 'out of
bounds for fourty foot length may serve . . .'[82]

The house's interior was planned on a magnificent scale. On the
ground floor were an axially placed hall and private dining room,
occupying the place and probably the function of the garden
parlour at Arniston and Yester. On the left of this dining-room
were the private drawing-room and cabinet. To its right and occupying the eastern third of the house were the family bedchamber
and dressing-rooms and closets for Lord and Lady Braco. The

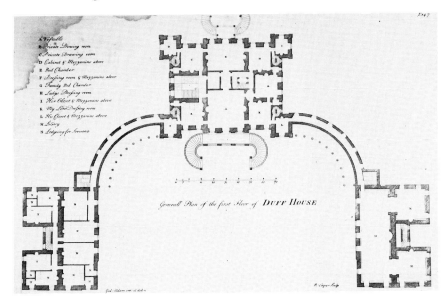

Duff House. Plan of
ground floor
(Vitruvius Scoticus)

great stair on the left of the hall led to the first floor where the space above the hall was occupied by the saloon, a thirty-foot cube with a coved ceiling rising into the attic. From the saloon an ante-chamber opened into the state drawing-room above the private dining-room. Each side of the saloon and state drawing-room was a suite of bedchamber, dressing-room and stool room, one of the apartments off the drawing-room presumably housing the state bedchamber.

The roof over the main block was completed in 1740 and work then stopped,[83] Adam later suing Lord Braco for payment for workmanship and materials. Most of the carved stone had been executed at Adam's own quarry at Queensferry, a proceeding approved by Lord Braco in 1737 when John Burt, the foreman mason at Duff House, informed Adam that:

> I told his Lordship that I was thinking it would be as good a way to let the Capitalls be done in the South Country rather than here on Account there were but two Carvers in the South Countrey that I know of could do the affair and that they lived South about Jedburgh So that it would be chargeable to bring them So far from home And if they were done at the Ferry you would have opportunity of Seeing them done both of the best Stone and true proportions . . . [84]

Duff House.
Pediment

The Jedburgh carvers were duly employed to carve the capitals, vases and coats of arms at Queensferry, the finished work then being shipped to Banff.[85] But the quality of carved stonework was insufficient to disabuse Lord Braco of the obsessive but ill-founded conviction which he came to feel that he had been cheated by William Adam. In consequence, according to his brother-in-law:

> he never occupied the house, and when obliged to drive past it on his way to Banff, always drew down the blinds of his coach.[86]

The judge who was eventually to hear William Adam's lawsuit against Lord Braco was himself one of Adam's clients. Andrew

Andrew Fletcher, Lord Milton, by Allan Ramsay

Fletcher, Lord Milton, the Lord Justice Clerk, was the principal Scottish agent for the management of both the financial and the political interests of the second Duke of Argyll and his brother the Earl of Ilay. By 1733 Milton had acquired Brunstane House near Edinburgh, one of the properties formerly owned by the Duke of Lauderdale for whom Sir William Bruce had remodelled the house. In 1734 Adam prepared drawings for a partial rebuilding and complete recasting of the mansion. He proposed the rebuilding of Bruce's south wing which had made the late sixteenth-century L-plan house into a U and the infilling of the court with a pedimented central block, an Imperial stair being stretched across its front. In its essentials this scheme was a return to the solution devised for explanding L-plan houses associated with John Mylne and Sir William Bruce in the 1660s. Adam's suggested front elevation was hardly more innovative, the wings being given shaped gables containing Gibbsian Venetian windows, and the centrepiece handled with understated blandness. Inside, the new centre block would have contained a two-storey hall, family rooms occupying the existing north and east ranges. In the new south range was to be a two-storey gallery, sixty-three feet long with each end marked off by a columned screen to form a cubic space. In the design of this gallery Adam showed some pride, asserting that it 'will make a fine room when the Cubes are sett off at the ends of the room with the pillars as proposed . . .'[87]

This scheme seems to have been too ambitious for Lord Milton who contented himself with a remodelling of the existing house executed under Adam's direction during the next few years. A major part in this remodelling was played by Thomas Clayton, who produced stucco enrichment of superb quality in the family bedchamber and the dressing-rooms provided for Lord Milton and his wife, while in the octagonal parlour he erected a high relief trophy above the fireplace. This enrichment extended even in to the dairy whose foliaged ceiling and marble floor suggest that it was intended for pleasure as much as utility.[88] A hint of the exasperation felt by an architect whose craftsmen were late in producing promised work is given in the letters Adam wrote about a painting, presumably for an overmantel, being copied by John Medina from an Aikman original. In May, 1736, he expected it 'soon'[89] but by August it was still not finished, causing him to complain to Lord Milton:

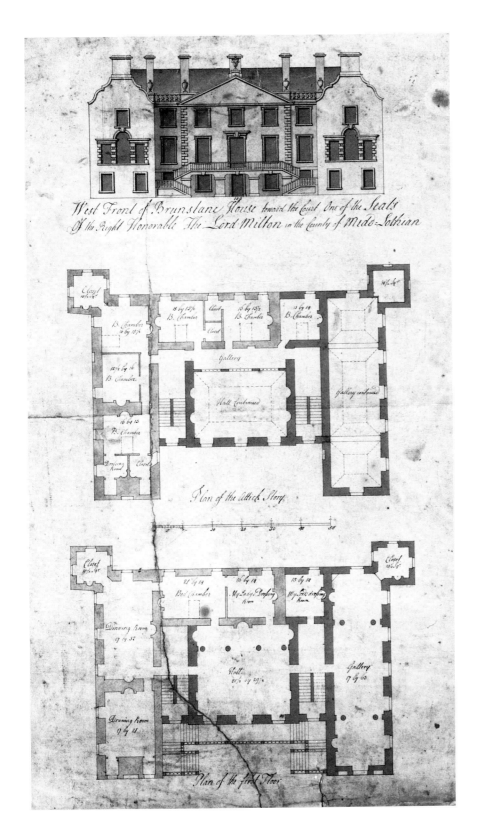

West Front of Brunslane House toward the Court One of the Seats
Of the Right Honorable The Lord Milton in the County of Mido-Lothian

Plan of the Attick Story

Plan of the first Floor

Brunstane House.
William Adam's
proposed elevation
and plan

I have so often teasd Mr Modena about the Picture & he so often promisd, that I know not what to say of him I wish yor Lo[rdshi]p would cause any of yor ser[van]ts call when they are goeing to Town possibly it may spurr him up. For Id have it rady befor I did the Marble Frame and other ornaments I propose for it.[90]

In 1740 Lord Milton's patron, John, second Duke of Argyll, bought Royston House and renamed it Caroline Park in honour of his daughter and heiress. His intention was not to have a showhouse so much as a suburban alternative to his apartment in the Palace of Holyroodhouse for use during his occasional visits to Edinburgh when he required:

a place fitt to retire to and do business in without being disturbed, which is impossible for him to do at the Abbay [Holyroodhouse] . . . [91]

Brunstane House.
Bedchamber

After the Duke's purchase of Caroline Park, William Adam was employed to add new offices and carry out a substantial amount of repair and minor alteration to the house.[92] The Duke was clearly regarded as a demanding client and Lord Milton was anxious to ensure that work was completed promptly. At the end of 1740 he sent a report to the Duke's agent in London detailing progress and concluding with the news that:

> Mr Adams says he had from his Grace to ye 1st. of May to have all finched, but as I know the laithers will always have most to do I inci[s]ted he was mistaken.th[a]t his Grace only allowed him to ye first of Appril. But all ye length I could bug him was to allow me to tell his Grace all shuld be finished by the middle of Aprile.[93]

Whether undertaken only as a speculative project or because of some commission from the Duke, William Adam also produced a scheme to remodel Caroline Park by the addition of a new Palladian fronted block to its entrance front. Externally, it would have been very smart, the broad central pediment filled with a huge heraldic achievement. Inside, the whole of the first floor was to have been filled by a gallery or 'Great room', a twenty-seven-foot-high triple cube.

Caroline Park (formerly Royston) House. William Adam's proposed front

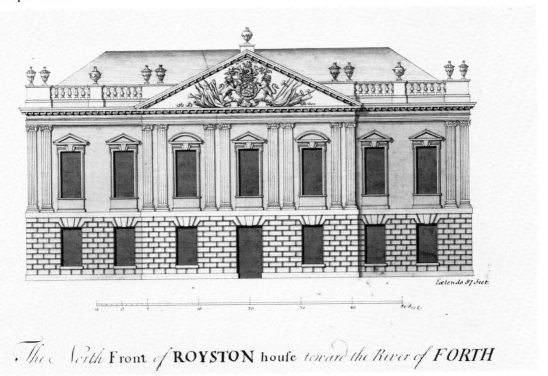

Extends 87 Feet.

The North Front of **ROYSTON** *houfe toward the River of* **FORTH**

Between 1725 and 1761 Archibald, Earl of Ilay, who succeeded his brother as Duke of Argyll in 1743, was the Scottish minister or 'manager' in the London government, organising Scottish members of Parliament and in charge of the distribution of government jobs and pensions in Scotland.[94] From 1729 the Earl laid out a model farm, dug drains and planted trees on his Peeblesshire estate of The Whim.[95] In March 1730, Ilay wrote from London to Lord Milton:

> Pray prepare me a plan of my farm house which I shall revise here & consult with the learned . . . [96]

The design was given Ilay's general approval in May,[97] but in August William Adam was suggesting amendments, writing to Lord Milton:

> I have taken the Liberty of giveing Yo[r]. Lordship this trouble, Being I had a Conversation with Scotstarvit Concerning the Ferm House Yo[r] Lo[rdshi]p designs for My Lord Islay, and upon his Scratching out the design, I propos'd Some Small alterations which he lik'd, and Said he believd they woud be acceptable to Yo[r] Lo[rdshi]p.[98]

The alterations proposed were indeed minor, but Adam does seem to have exercised some general superintendence over the building of the house. In May, 1732, he wrote from The Whim to Lord Milton:

> As the masson here was at a loss how to dispose the First Storie of the House Major Cochran desir'd me to make a step out in order to give directions about it, and accordingly is done by a Plan of it left with him, pointing out the places of Chimneys doors windows &c[a]. with there Sizes and distances Set down in figures So as the masson Cannot mistake.[99]

In 1733-4 Samuel Calderwood, one of Adam's team of plasterers, was engaged on work at the house,[100] and a memorandum of 1733 noted that Adam was to be consulted 'about the Chimneys, and the dinning room'.[101]

On succeeding to his brother's dukedom in 1733 Lord Ilay inherited vast estates in Argyll and Dunbartonshire which, however, lacked a house of even moderate comfort, far less one suitable for a grandee. In England he had employed the Palladian

South Front of Inverary Castle the Seat of His Grace the Duke of Argyll in the County of Argyll

Roger Morris to design his seat at Whitton Place in Middlesex and
perhaps also Argyll House in London[102] and it was to Morris that
he turned for a design for a new castle at Inveraray on Loch Fyne
and perhaps also for the additions he proposed to build at
Rosneath at the mouth of Gare Loch. In August 1744, Morris
dined at Edinburgh with William Adam,[103] doubtless to discuss
the proposals. Preliminary work on the great castellated house at
Inveraray, a symbolic assertion of the still quasi-feudal power
exercised by the Duke of Argyll over the inhabitants within his
heritable jurisdictions, was begun in January 1745, when 1,000
fir trees were felled for scaffolding. By June, seventy-six men were
labouring at the foundations, at transporting timber and at quarrying.[104] The Jacobite rising of 1745–6 jolted the project's progress and in July, 1746, the Duke's agent Archibald Campbell was
clearly of the opinion that firmer control was required. He recommended the employment of:

> an Intendant General who shall direct the execution of the work,
> engage the tradesmen, settle their prices and draw their pay and
> keep accounts of the different branches of the work. This

Inveraray Castle
(Vitruvius Scoticus)

Intendant should be answerable that everything be done sufficiently and conform to the plan. Without such a person I am very
apprehensive things may go to confusion and that your Grace may
not have the satisfaction you justly must expect. I also incline to
think the Intendant should be a man of the first form for
experience and taste in building. Such a man must know the best
tradesmen, can hire them at a lower figure than any gentlemen
can do . . . If you have not already some other person in view, you
know that Mr Adams the architect is considered as the ablest man
we have in Scotland for carrying out so great a design. If Mr Adams
would take charge, he or his son might visit the work monthly
from March till November, stay here as long as necessary and leave
the proper directions till their return.[105]

This suggestion was adopted and from the autumn of 1746
William Adam acted as executant architect for Inveraray, cor-
responding directly with Morris about the work.[106] To achieve
satisfactory organisation on the site was difficult and when Adam,
Morris and the Duke together visited Inveraray in the autumn of
1747 it was clear that there was evidence of fraud and that yet
tighter control was necessary. By the time of his death in 1748
William Adam had established only the framework of a system
of proper supervision and accounting for the work which was to
be completed by his eldest son John over the next eleven
years.[107]

Chapter 8

ADAM'S PUBLIC BUILDINGS

W illiam Adam's architectural reputation, coupled with his ability as a contractor to undertake sizeable jobs, made him Scotland's foremost designer of public buildings in the early eighteenth century. In 1729 he was employed by Aberdeen Burgh Council to enlarge their Town House.[1] The next public building for which William Adam was responsible was also in Aberdeen where, on 19 September 1730, Robert Gordon, a merchant who had acquired a substantial fortune in Danzig,[2] signed a codicil to his will by which he left to the Town Council and ministers of Aberdeen the sum of £10,000 for the foundation of a 'hospital' or charity school for the children of impoverished burgesses of the town.[3] Two days later Gordon made an agreement to acquire a site from the Council, but this transaction had apparently not been completed by the time of his death the next year and so the feu charter of 1732 was granted by the Councillors to themselves and the burgh's ministers as Governors of Robert Gordon's Hospital.[4] At the same time the Governors bought an adjoining plot from Marischal College, the charter for this purchase stating that they had:

> been considering and looking for proper ground whereupon they might build the said Hospital and lay out the gardens, and they employed Mr. William Adams, the most celebrated architect in this Kingdom, to get his advice where it is proper to build the said Hospital and lay out the gardens, and to get a plan from him . . . [5]

The building was begun in 1732 and its shell completed the same year, although it then remained unoccupied except as a billet for Hanoverian troops during the Jacobite rising until 1750, probably because of the stipulation in Gordon's will that the annual income of the mortification was to amount to £6,000 Scots (£500 sterling) before any boy were admitted.[6] Adam's design produced a building of sober worth in the Gibbsian Palladian manner, dignified by a steeple taken from Gibbs' design for the Marylebone Chapel placed above the centre pediment. Similarly

South Front of Gordons Hospital att Aberdeen

Robert Gordon's Hospital (Vitruvius Scoticus)

Gibbsian in inspiration and with a very similar pediment but its steeple taken from Gibbs' design for St Martin-in-the-Fields, was Adam's Town House at Dundee built in 1732–4. This was a much more expensively detailed work with channelled rustication across the arcaded ground floor and with oval second-floor windows to light the two-storey Council House and Guild Room in the ends and the debtors's cells in the centre.

A third public building begun by Adam in 1732 was the Glasgow University Library. In 1720, after his sons had returned from a Scottish tour during which they had been hospitably received by the

Dundee Town House

Universtity of Glasgow, the Duke of Chandos had given £500 to the University, leaving it to the Duke of Montrose, the University's Chancellor, to decide how the money should be spent.[7] In 1726 Montrose concluded that the money which had been earning interest meanwhile should go to build a new library although he agreed to allow the faculty to postpone the work for a further three years if the amount were not yet sufficient. It was not however until 1731 that the faculty resolved to ask the Glasgow wrights Allan Dreghorn and John Craig to produce plans and estimates,[8] but these were rejected the next year in favour of a design by William

Glasgow University
Library. Contract
elevation by William
Adam

Section of the Coledge Library at GLASGOW

Gul Adam inv et delin   R. Cooper Sculp

Adam,[9] for which the foundation stone was laid by 27 June 1732, although completion of the building was to take another twelve years.[10] The library was a classy temple of learning. From the pedimented front projected a small Corinthian portico flanked by niches for statues and approached by a perron masking the high basement. The deeply cut coat of arms of the Duke of Chandos in the pediment, rusticated quoins and carved swags made a display of the mason's art, quite un-Palladian in spirit. The interior was expensive but disconcerting. The plan was essentially of a nave with narrow aisles, but the left aisle consisted only of one Ionic column at each end while the coved main ceiling spanned

from the basket-arched right arcade across this 'aisle' to the left wall.

Between 1734 and 1748 William Adam was responsible for the design of three of eighteenth-century Edinburgh's major buildings, all erected for charitable purposes. On 28 June 1734, several years after a subscription list had been opened, the foundation stone was laid of the Orphan Hospital.[11] intended for 'the bringing up of Orphans in the Principles of the Christian Religion, and for instructing them in Manufacture of Woolen and Linen'.[12] Not surprisingly the design was economical but Adam provided a centrepiece whose pediment rises against a cupolaed domed roof like a half-starved version of Vaux-le-Vicomte. The hospital was completed by 1736,[13] although an appeal for more donations had to be made in 1735 after the first stage was built, it being pointed out that in that work:

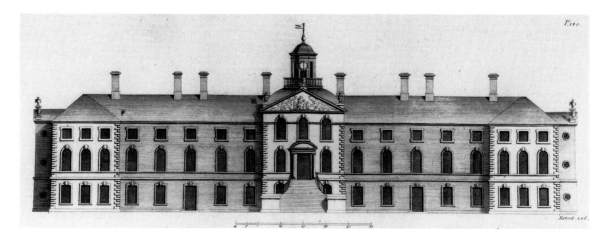

Orphan Hospital
(Vitruvius Scoticus)

some Journeymen Masons served as Volunteers, and only got their Meat. The Deacon of the Sclaters, and others of his Trade, bestowed Sclates; and he, with some of his Trade, caused cover the said Roof; and a Plumber did his Part, as to Work, all *gratis*: And some of the Timber-merchants did very generously give largely to this Work; and 'tis expected, that the Wrights and Glasiers will contribute in their Way, towards this Undertaking.[14]

On his death in 1723 George Watson, an Edinburgh merchant who had become the first accountant of the Bank of Scotland, left £144,000 Scots (£12,000 sterling) to the Merchants' Company,[15] who were to act as his trustees:

> to raise a new Hospitall for entertaining and educating of the male children and grandchildren of decayed merchants in Edinburgh . . .[16]

A site for this charity school was acquired in Thomson's Yards at the south-east corner of the burgh but no building work had taken place by 1736 when a committee of the Governors presented the Trustees with a 'Memorial' advocating that a site off what is now Lauriston Place just outside the town walls should be preferred. They argued that the Thomson's Yards site was too small and that its location was:

> interjected between the Colledge and High School, which should the Hospital be built there, would expose the boys to the hazard of the insults of both; as well as being let into their vices, and here the Committee beg leave to notice a general observation, that the

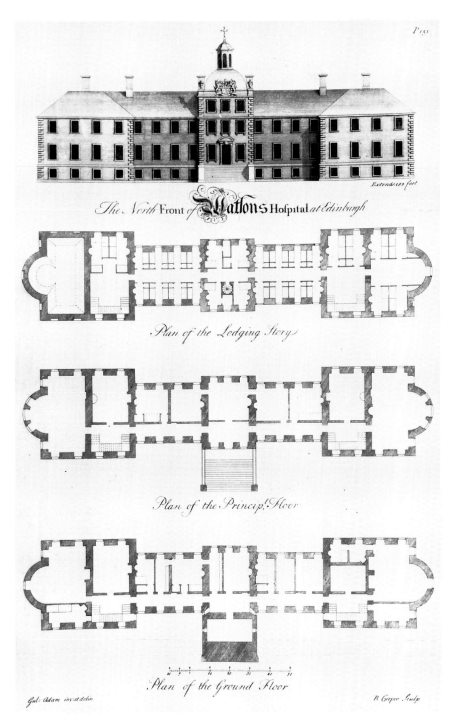

The North Front of Watsons Hospital at Edinburgh

Plan of the Lodging Story

Plan of the Princip.l Floor

Plan of the Ground Floor

vices of the Boys of Herriot's Hospital have been much owing to their being situate so near the Grass Mercate, who being despised by the better sort as Charity Boys, ly under too great a temptation of taking up with mean and wicked boys . . .[17]

George Watson's Hospital (Vitruvius Scoticus)

In 1738 the Thomson's Yards site was sold to the Trustees of the
Royal Infirmary and the Lauriston Place site acquired instead.[18]
William Adam's estimate and design, accepted by the management committee in the same year, were for a variant on his
Orphans' Hospital design, the front elevation even starker and the
centrepiece deprived of its pediment but carried up a storey
higher to make a tower, possibly in allusion to the similar tower
over the entrance to George Heriot's Hospital. Inside, George
Watson's Hospital seems to have been less severe than the
Orphans' Hospital, having a chapel at one end and a large dining
room at the other although for the second floor Adam prudently
specified deal partitions, observing that:

> These partitions are thought more propper in deal than in Lath
> & plaister, As the plaister would be subject to be much broke by
> the boys . . . [19]

Royal Infirmary   The Royal Infirmary whose Trustees bought the Thomson's

Yards site in 1738 had been established by subscription in the
1720s, a house being adapted as a temporary hospital in 1729,
and a charter of incorporation granted by George II in 1736.[20] On
acquiring this new site William Adam was immediately
appointed architect for the proposed permanent hospital, the
managers stating in the report for 1738 that:

> they ought in forming the plan to have regard not only to their
> Capital Stock at present but to what it may be increased to in future
> ages. That therefore the building ought to be solid and erected of
> the most durable materials, not slovenly, and yet that very little or
> no expense should be laid out in useless ornament . . . [21]

For this large U-plan edifice Adam duly pared down ornament to
the minimum except at the centrepiece which was a much more
opulent version of the Orphans' Hospital and George Watson's
Hospital type, of five bays instead of three, with attached Ionic
columns and deeply carved Mannerist scrolls flanking the attic.
The foundation stone was laid on 2 August 1738,[22] and, according
to *The Caledonian Mercury*:

> Several Societies and Persons of Condition made large Contribu-
> tions upon this Occasion for the Carrying on of the Work,
> Gentlemen Proprietors of Stone-Quarries having made presents
> of Stones, others of Lime, Merchants have given considerable
> Parcels of Timber, the Wrights and Masons have contributed
> largely, the Farmers in the Neighbourhood have agreed to carry
> all Materials gratis, the Journeymen Masons are to contribute their
> Labour in furnishing each a certain Quantity of hewn Stones. And
> as this Undertaking is for the Relief of the Diseased, lame and
> maimed Poor, even the Day-Labourers employed have agreed to
> work a Day in each Month gratis.[23]

The first patients were admitted in 1741 and the building completed in 1748, the year of Adam's death.[24] Inside, the ground
floor contained a great entrance hall with the central main stair
at its back, kitchen and storage accommodation, rooms for staff,
twelve cells for lunatics, and hot and cold baths.[25] On the upper
floors the wards stretched out each side from the main stair
which, according to a description of 1739:

> has a large Lant in the Middle, by which it is proposed that a Patient
> may be carried by a Pully in a Chair to all the different Galleries,

to prevent to racking Pain that might otherwise be occasioned in being carried up or down Stairs.[26]

On the first floor, the front room in the centre was the Managers' Room, its coffered ceiling enriched with stucco rosettes and trophies. Above the fireplace was a stucco relief of Charity to remind the managers of their good work. On the top floor above the stair was the operating theatre, a thirty foot cube rising into the attic,[27] 'where more than 200 Students can see Operations, and which is also a convenient *Chapel*.'[28] The cupola above was 'sometimes employed as an *Astronomical Observatory*.'[29]

*Royal Infirmary,
Managers' Room*

William Adam's posts as Clerk and Storekeeper of the Works in Scotland and Mason to the Board of Ordnance in North Britain were not sinecures. He was called on by the Court of Exchequer to report on the condition of buildings for whose maintenance the Government was responsible. In 1729 he sent Sir John Clerk a memorandum about the state of the Bishop's Palace in Glasgow, 'which yor Lo[rdshi]p may please to Considder and lay befor the other Barrons of Exchequer.'[30] After examining the roof of the Palace of Holyroodhouse in 1733 Adam reported that £4,000 worth of repairs was necessary, in response to which the Barons of Exchequer made £3,000 available.[31] In the same year he acted for the Board of Ordnance as both designer and contractor for the five-arch bridge over the Tay at Aberfeldy, whose obelisk-topped cutwaters give an architectural elegance to a structure whose purpose was primarily to serve the needs of the army.[32] After suppression of the Jacobite rising of 1745–6 the military contracts increased. In 1746 Adam was paid for 'workmanship and repairs performed and materials delivered' at Fort Augustus, Blackness Castle, Carlisle, Dumbarton Castle, Edinburgh Castle, Stirling Castle, Fort William and Duart Castle.[33] At Edinburgh Castle in 1747 he began a new powder magazine which was to be finished after his death at a cost of about £1,380.[34] 1747 was also the year in which he was awarded the contract to build a new fort at Inverness. Before work began the site was switched to Ardersier

Tay Bridge, Aberfeldy

Fort George

Point where the building of the huge Fort George started in 1748, the project being completed by Adam's sons more than ten years later.[35]

Involvement with the Army even affected William Adam's social life, at times causing him to neglect civilian patrons. In 1735 he had to write to Lord Milton to apologise for having missed an appointment:

> But Capt[ain]Romer ane Engineer in the office of ordnance who I am oblig'd to attend came to John Walls this day & din'd and after drinking a hearty Glass, I found it necessary to step forward this length [to Tranent] with him & keep him all night so that I begg your Lordship will excuse me . . . .[36]

Chapter 9

BURGESS OF EDINBURGH AND
LAIRD OF BLAIR ADAM

When William Adam moved his family to Edinburgh after Robert's birth in July 1728, he set up house in a property on the south side of the Cowgate adjoining buildings belonging to the Incorporation of Mary's Chapel. He had some problems with the Incorporation about the upkeep of the close which served both his property and theirs, writing to their boxmaster or treasurer in January, 1733:

> As to the Closs I believe all will be easily Convinced that there is much need for new paveing it, for the common benefit of both your houses & mine wherefore should be glad you would appoint your own mason to do it & I shall pay any proportion of the Expence that you & the other members shall think reasonable . . . [1]

By the end of December Adam was querying his proportion of the cost of paving but 'signefied that he would not differ with the Incorporation in that matter'.[2] Two years later he wrote to the Incorporation's boxmaster to complain about his neighbours occupying flats or houses belonging to the Incorporation and suggested the obvious remedy to the problem:

> You will remember on thursday last and above seven moneths ago I spoke to you Concerning the Inconveniencies M[r] Johnston's family & mine were brought under by the two litle Tennants in the Closs, As I told you before what these Inconveniences were I need not relate them now, But were you to make a Stepp down att this present would give a full prooff of what I have said But to remedy all I hereby renew my former proposall of renting both the Houses from you & pay the same Rent that those Tennants now do, By which means M[r] Johnston & I can have such Neighbours as is agreeable to us and I hope, you'l think your rent as good by me as those that possess it.[3]

At the same time he referred to another matter of contention although stating:

I shall not now Complain of the Stones that are lying in the Entry because on Thursday last you told me there was orders to remove them.[4]

On his Cowgate property William Adam built a new tenement, clearly of considerable size and quality since the flat occupied by Sir Robert Henderson of Fordell in 1745 contained on one floor a dining-room, drawing-room, five bedrooms and closets, a kitchen and pantry, and had also two cellars and three attic rooms,[5] making it larger than the smart little town house which Adam had built for the judge, Lord Minto.[6] On the opposite side of the Cowgate Adam leased the old Leather Market as a coalyard.[7] In 1734 he bought lofts and granaries in Leith and expanded his property there five years later, probably as a store for building materials and those marble chimneypieces of which he was a frequent purveyor.[8]

Just outside Edinburgh William Adam had bought the small estate of North Merchiston, probably in 1726,[9] where he seems to have let the house and planted the parkland.[10] In 1731 he made a much larger acquisition, buying the lands of Blair Crambeth in Kinross-shire for £8,010 Scots (£667 10s. sterling),[11] these then consisting of 817 acres.[12] To these between 1739 and 1747 he added adjoining estates,[13] ending with a total of over 3,000 acres.[14] When Adam bought Blair Crambeth (soon renamed Blair Adam) it was, according to his grandson, an example of land untouched by agricultural improvement:

All, except the 20 or 30 Acres of the infield land, was a wild uncultivated Moor, covered either with heather or coarse russet

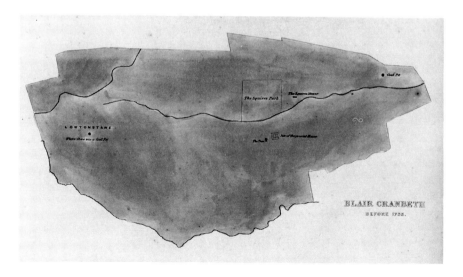

Blair Adam, c. 1730

grass; and in the wettest parts, with sprats and rushes . . . with the exception of the two small pieces of infield land, there was not a vestige of culture, nor a tree, except one accidental Ash Tree . . . [15]

From 1733 Adam began improvement of the estate, making enclosures, planting trees and introducing better quality live-stock.[16] Since there was no habitable dwelling, he built a modest house, half of which was occupied by a resident factor, the other half used by himself on his occasional visits.[17] When, a few years later, he bought the adjoining lands of Woodend he acquired 'a Mansion House . . . which had trees and walks around it, suitable to the residence of a Scottish Gentleman of that period' but this he left to go to ruin. The further extension of his property by the

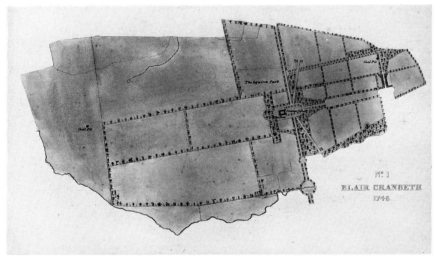

Blair Adam in 1748

William Adam's house at Blair Adam

purchase of Dowhill to the north brought him 'a Castle, which in 1740, was fit for the habitation of a Gentleman's family', but he again refused to set himself up as a laird and converted the building into labourers' accommodation.[18] On the east edge of the Blair Adam estate was a workable coal seam which Adam mined,[19] and for whose colliers he founded a village named Maryburgh in honour of his wife.[20] Blair Adam seems to have been used as a rural retreat by William Adam only during the Jacobite rising of 1745 when he thought it prudent to retire there from Edinburgh, accompanied by his eldest son John and two of his brothers-in-law.[21]

Involvement in coal mining, both on his own account and as an adviser to others, had probably been part of William Adam's business activity since he first entered into partnership with William Robertson at Linktown of Abbotshall. Among the accounts outstanding at Adam's death was the sum of £200 owed him by the Duke of Hamilton for:

> His pains going frequently to Borrowstoness during the Course of six years superintending the fitting of the Coal and salt works & erecting the fire Engine . . .[22]

In 1736, when his lease on the Cockenzie coal mines and salt pans came to an end,[23] Adam considered bidding for a new lease but, as he explained to Lord Milton:

> If I cou'd have it at ane easy rent So as to be in a Condition to Compence Some part of a great deall of money I have lost by it woud be lucky; But as my old friend Mr Buchan has a Notion that a great deall of money is to be made by it, I am affraid he'l put it out of my power to take it, I am fully satisfyd he will Burn his fingers, But then, I shall lose the opportunity of getting any part of my loss made up.[24]

Three years later Adam took a lease of the Marquess of Tweeddale's coalfield at Pinkie.[25] There he first used a horse-powered pump to drain water from the seams but found this 'both inconvenient and too expensive'. Consequently, in 1742–4, he made a canal to bring water from the Esk to the foot of the hill on which stands Inveresk Church and bored a six-foot-high pipe through the hill to carry the water to power the pumping machinery for the mine.[26] It was in connection with his work and possible damage to the land above that Lord Tweeddale was warned by his factor Thomas Hay that in any negotiation:

> Your Lordship knows that Mr Adams is very sly & has abundance of smooth things to say & manadges his point of view with prudence & adress . . . [27]

William Adam's lease of stone quarries at Queensferry probably began as a part of his work at the nearby Hopetoun House. However, their main importance to him was as a source of top quality stone for carving and, since they were situated conveniently near the Forth, finished pieces could be shipped to buildings for which Adam was the contractor. As he explained in the course of his lawsuit with Lord Braco:

> . . . he took a lease of the quarries at the Queensferry which every body knew produced Freestone of the best kind, and finest grain of any in Scotland by which means he was enabled from thence to furnish the best of Stones for the finest pieces of any work that he was imployed to execute in all the different parts of the Countrey where there was conveniency of Transporting the Same by Sea Carriage.[28]

The project for publishing a *Vitruvius Scoticus* was, despite the shortage of subscribers, pursued in the 1730s. The Yorkshire-born engraver Richard Cooper had settled in Edinburgh by 1729 when he was among the signatories to the indenture founding a short-lived Academy of St Luke, its other members including William Adam, the older and younger Allan Ramsay, two of the Norie family, and the portraitist John Alexander.[29] Cooper's first engravings for *Vitruvius Scoticus* were probably executed in 1730 and he continued to engrave Adam's designs for the rest of the decade.[30] The project may then have lapsed, although Adam's surviving elevation and plan of Caroline Park, drawn as if for an engraver, cannot be earlier than 1740.[31] It may have been revived shortly before or after William Adam's death, some of the printed plates being on paper made at The Hague in 1746.[32]

William Adam's life in the 1740s was dogged by his dispute with Lord Braco about payment for work at Duff House, Adam initiating proceedings in 1741 for the sum of £5,796 12s 11⅓d. which he claimed was owed him. The principal point at issue was whether Adam had been contractor for the mason work as well as the architect.[33] There is little doubt that Adam was in the right.

What is less clear is whether Lord Braco had genuinely
misunderstood Adam's position or whether, because of some
falling out, he had determined to try to ruin the architect. Braco's
character was described sympathetically, but revealingly, by his
brother-in-law William Baird:

> He had inflexible principles of honour and justice from which
> nothing could make him depart but misinformation or prejudice,
> which last, if once he had contracted it against any person, it was
> not easy to remove, especially if he thought he had met with any
> Disingenuity, or been in the least imposed upon.[34]

That Braco was disputatious is not in doubt, for as Baird observed:

> He also spent much in Lawsuits and in political disputes, for when
> he once took a cause in hand he spared no cost to carry it through.[35]

During his career Braco fought cases against the Duke of Gordon,
the Earl of Findlater, Lord Banff and the burgh of Banff, as well
as against Adam and others.[36] In the course of the lawsuit with
William Adam, Braco seems to have been convinced of his own
rectitude. At one point he wrote to his wife from Edinburgh:

> Col[one]l Abercromby proposes to set out to-morrow, your
> brother goes to Hopetoun, everybodie gets their feet loose except
> me, who have been so imborrowed with my own blunder of having
> to do with Adam . . . I don't blame myself for anything that has hap-
> pened, except that I was so unluckie as to put trust in a fellow that
> has turned out as great a rogue as ever was on earth. Who indeed
> had supporters as void of conscience as himself.[37]

The case was heard in the Court of Session in 1743 when
William Adam was reported to have spoken 'with so much elo-
quence and impressive energy that it had a powerful effect upon
the court and very much contributed to the success of his cause'.[38]
The judge, who found substantially in Adam's favour, was Lord
Milton, his patron, former client and a friend from whom he had
previously borrowed architectural publications including a 'Book
of Pallaces' and 'That on the Stadt house of Amst[erdam]'.[39] Lord
Braco may have had some justification for his comment that
'There never was a judge did show more partiality than the
Justice Clerk . . .'[40]

Proceedings continued almost to the very end of Adam's life, Lord Braco making pugnacious use of the legal devices open to someone with a great deal of money at his disposal. When, in December, 1747, during a temporary respite from the 'long and severe indisposition' which was to prove his final illness, Adam heard that an interlocutory judgment was likely to be issued against him at Braco's instigation, he wrote to Lord Milton:

> The near view I have lately had of going out of the World, & leaving my Family to struggle thro' an intricate affair of such importance to them, and when I must be sencible they had so powerful an Antagonist to engage with, has greatly heighten'd my disquiet on Acco^t of every appearance of Spineing out this affair beyond the term of my Life, which by the Shock I have sustain'd has become greatly more precarious. And indeed my Good Lord, it is not without reason that I dread this to be Lord Braco's cheiff aim, because at the very beginning of our differences, he thought he could not terrify me more effectually than by avowing his resolution, To tyre me out & break me.[41]

Milton's own illness at the time added to Adam's concern:

> Your Lo[rdshi]p is better able to judge than I how dismal the consequences would be to me & my Family, if it should prevent You from giving the finishing Stroke to this matter yourself.[42]

Four days later Adam declared himself ready to yield some ground to Lord Braco, hoping to gain forgiveness from Milton for the trouble he was causing him:

> by making whatever concessions are in my power, in order to bring the difference betwixt Lord Braco & me to a speedy determination, & to have the matter struck off; provided only they are such as do not bring me under the reproach of having hurt my numerous family, by too tamely yeilding what appear'd a most just Claim. For this reason, my Good Lord, I do not think it enough that I have put myself into Your hands, in hope of Your Lo[rdshi]p saving me from being wronged; Unless I also declare my readiness to acquiesce chearfully in every healling overture Your Lo[rdshi]p may judge propper to propose, tho' at the expence of yeilding something, which I might carry if I was a match for my Antagonist either in wealth or in obstinacy.[43]

The case was finally settled very soon after but Lord Braco

remained vindictive. At the end of January 1748, after Lord
Milton had sent a servant 'to know if I was alive', Adam wrote to
the judge:

> I was indeed at first a little surpriz'd at the message, but sometime
> after a Gentleman came to see me, who also said he had heard I
> was dead. My Son had also a Letter from another Gentleman on
> the same subject, & we find this news took its rise in my Freind
> Lord Braco's. This in appearance to me is but a poor peice of
> revenge, But I thank God I am yet alive, & some [sic.] stronger
> than when I had the honour to see Your Lo[rdshi]p last.[44]

William Adam's family became numerous. A third son James

*John Adam, by
Francis Cotes*

was born in 1732 and a fourth William in 1738, as well as five more daughters whose dates of birth have not been recorded.[45] John, the eldest son, was sent to Dalkeith Grammar School, almost certainly attended at the same time by Robert Smith, later to be the leading architect in Philadelphia, and then spent a short time at Edinburgh University before being removed by his father to assist him in his architectural and contracting practice. Robert went to the Edinburgh High School at the early age of six and then followed his brother to the University, apparently also leaving prematurely in 1746 and joining the family's firm.[46] When the Master Carpenter to the Board of Ordnance died in 1746 William Adam was quick to put his twenty-five-year-old eldest son's name forward for the post, writing to Lord Milton from Inveraray:

> I am advis'd from Edin[r] this day, that Mr Mowbray who was Master Carpenter to the Board of Ordnance, died the 21st Curr[t]. I am sorry for his death, but as no doubt somebody will be soon applying for his bussines, and that my son John has been bred up in the knowledge of Carpenter work, as well as mason's work & Architecture, I should gladely wish to have him succeed M[r] Mowbray in that Office.[47]

That attempt to obtain a Government post for John Adam was unsuccessful but William Adam was well justified in praising his children's accomplishments if the portrait given of the family by John Clerk of Eldin is at all trustworthy:

> The numerous family of M[r] Adam, now grown up, the uninterrupted cordiality in which they lived, their conciliating manners, & the various accomplishments in which they had severally made proficiency, formed a most attractive society, & failed not to draw around them a set of men, whose learning, & genius have since done honor to that country which gave them birth. Amongst these were Doctor Robertson the Historian, allied to the Adams by consanguinity, Doctor Drysdale Author of Sermons, John Clerk Esquire Author of Naval Tactics, both allied to this family by marriage, Doctor Adam Smith Author of the Wealth of Nations, David Hume Esquire the Historian, John Home Esquire Author of Tragedies, Doctor Adam Fergusson Historian & Author of the progress of civil Society, Doctor William Wilkie Author of the Epigoniad, Doctor John Blair Author of the Chronology Doctor John Hutton Author of the Theory of the Earth, & many others whose superior taste & genius have since been displayed in

Robert Adam, by
James Tassie

elegant & useful works which have rendered their names immortal.[48]

William Adam fell ill in the autumn of 1747 and at last, on 24 June 1748, he died of a:

> suppression of urine—the last he passed was black like Ink—he was affected with a swelling not only in his belly, but his right hand; when the swelling abated and not till then his head was affected [he] lost his senses and did not live many hours.[49]

Six days later *The Caledonian Mercury* published an obituary:

> On Friday last died Mr. WILLIAM ADAM Architect, generally lamented, and deservedly so, not only by those who knew him, but by all who wish well to the Publick. His Genius for Architecture push'd him out of Obscurity into a high Degree of Reputation. And his Activity of Spirit, not to be confined within narrow Bounds,

*William Adam's
Mausoleum, by
James Adam*

diffused itself into many Branches of Business, not more to his own
Benefit than that of his native Country. As to the latter, 'tis

fortunate he has left behind him some promising young Men, to carry on what he has so happily begun. Their Regard for so worthy a Man, their Parent, will be to them a more than ordinary Incitement to tread in his Steps; for he was a good Artist, but still a better Man.[50]

He was buried at Edinburgh in Greyfriars' Churchyard, where five years later his sons erected a mausoleum over the grave. Within this domed Roman temple William Adam is commemorated by an inscription tablet carved with his portrait. Below the tablet is a tomb chest, its front bearing a relief of his design for Hopetoun House, his intended portico in ruins on the ground serving as a *memento mori*.

CHAPTER 1

1. T. C. Smout, *Scottish Trade on the Eve of Union* (Edinburgh and London, 1963), 2 and n.

2. James Handley, *Scottish Farming in the Eighteenth Century* (London, 1953), 52.

3. *Ibid.*, 46-7.

4. *Ibid.*, 57-65.

5. *Ibid.*, 38-42.

6. Gordon Donaldson, *Scotland: James V to James VII* (Edinburgh and London, 1965), 386-7; T. C. Smout and Alexander Fenton, 'Scottish Agriculture before the Improvers – an Exploration', *The Agricultural History Review*, xiii (1965), 82-4.

7. National Library of Scotland, Adv. MS 33.5.16, Sir Robert Sibbald, 'Discourse Anent the Improvements may be made in Scotland for advancing the Wealth of the Kingdome', 12 September, 1698, 86.

8. Smout, *op. cit.*, 6-8.

9. Handley, *op. cit.*, 45.

10. *Ibid.*, 55-6.

11. *Ibid.*, 158-9 and n.; but they were grown for human consumption, *see* Rosalind Marshall, *The Days of Duchess Anne* (London, 1973), 52.

12. William Ferguson, *Scotland: 1689 to the Present* (Edinburgh and London, 1968), 79. Salt beef was one of the staple dishes on gentry tables in winter during the early eighteenth century according to John Ramsay of Ochtertyre, *Scotland and Scotsmen in the Eighteenth Century*, ed. Alexander Allardyce, ii (Edinburgh, 1888), 69.

13. Smout, *op. cit.*, 237.

14. *Ibid.*, 213.

15. Ferguson, *op. cit.*, 80.

16. *Ibid.*, 80.

17. N.L.S., Adv. MS 33.5.16, 80.

18. Handley, *op. cit.*, 55.

19. *Ibid.*, 62.

20. Smout and Fenton, *op. cit.*, 74.

21. Andrew Fletcher, *The Political Works* (London, 1732), 156; Smout and Fenton, *op. cit.*, 74.

22. Smout and Fenton, *op. cit.*, 74.

23. Handley, *op. cit.*, 83-6.

24. *Ibid.*, 47.

25. *Ibid.*, 89; Ferguson, *op. cit.*, 78.

26. *Early Travellers in Scotland*, ed. P. Hume Brown (Edinburgh, 1891), 261. By the early seventeenth century the Baron Courts could pass sentence of death only on a murderer caught in the act or a thief found with stolen property in his or her possession; *see* J. A. Symon, *Scottish Farming* (Edinburgh and London, 1959), 41.

27. Ferguson, *op. cit.*, 73-4.

28. (William Mackintosh of Borlum). *An Essay on Ways and Means for Inclosing, Fallowing, Planting, &c. Scotland* (Edinburgh, 1729), 2-4, 117.

29. Handley, *op. cit.*, 87-8.

30. Fletcher, *op. cit.*, 155-6.

31. Donaldson, *op. cit.*, 240.

32. Fletcher, *op. cit.*, 145; N.L.S., Adv. MS 33.5.16, 88.

33. N.L.S., Adv. MS 33.5.16, 88.

34. Fletcher, *op. cit.*, 144; N.L.S., Adv. MS 33.5.16, 88.

35. Ferguson, *op. cit.*, 79.

36. Smout and Fenton, *op. cit.*, 98.

37. *Acts of the Parliaments of Scotland*, ix (1822), 421.

38. Handley, *op. cit.*, 117-22.

39. *Ibid.*, 145-8.

40. [William Mackintosh of Borlum], *op. cit.*, xliii.

41. *Ibid.*, xlvi.

42. *Ibid.*, xlvii.

43. Ferguson, *op. cit.*, 167.

44. [William Adam], *Progress of an Estate in Scotland* [Blair Adam, c. 1835], 7.

45. Ferguson, *op. cit.*, 81.

46. *Early Travellers in Scotland*, 275.

47. A.I. Bowman, 'Culross Colliery: a Sixteenth-Century Mine', *Industrial Archaeology*, vii (1970), 356–68.

48. Smout, *op. cit.*, 74.

49. R. Page Arnot, *A History of the Scottish Miners* (London, 1955), 4–6.

50. Bowman, *op. cit.*, 356–7.

51. Donaldson, *op. cit.*, 246.

52. *The Acts of the Parliaments of Scotland*, x (1823), 267.

53. Ferguson, *op. cit.*, 81, 186–7.

54. *Early Travellers in Scotland*, 276.

55. Smout, *op. cit.*, 227.

56. *Ibid.*, 8, 231–2.

57. *Ibid.*, 219–24.

58. *The Register of the Privy Council of Scotland*, 3rd series, vii (Edinburgh, 1915), 495.

59. Smout, *op. cit.*, 234–6.

60. Ferguson, *op. cit.*, 180.

61. Smout, *op. cit.*, 233.

62. Alastair J. Durie, *The Scottish Linen Industry in the Eighteenth Century* (Edinburgh, 1979), 9.

63. Ferguson, *op. cit.*, 180–1.

64. Durie, *op. cit.*, 37.

65. *Ibid.*, 55.

66. Ferguson, *op. cit.*, 181–2.

67. Durie, *op. cit.*, 22.

68. Ferguson, *op. cit.*, 182.

69. T. C. Smout, 'The Development and Enterprise of Glasgow', *Scottish Journal of Political Economy*, vii (1960), 194.

70. Ferguson, *op. cit.*, 85.

71. William Mackay Mackenzie, *The Scottish Burghs* (Edinburgh and London, 1949), 80.

72. One hundred and eleven were created, 1660–1707. *See* George Smith Pryde, *The Burghs of Scotland* (London, Glasgow and New York, 1965), 71–80.

73. Robert Dick, *Annals of Colinsburgh* (Edinburgh, 1896), 54.

74. Smout, 'The Development and Enterprise of Glasgow', 204.

75. Smout, *Scottish Trade on the Eve of Union*, 17.

76. N.L.S., MS 1749, f.1, John Cadell to John Gray, 17 September, 1748.

77. Smout, *Scottish Trade on the Eve of Union*, 77–8.

78. *The Register of the Privy Council of Scotland*, 3rd series, vi (Edinburgh, 1914), 9.

79. *The Register of the Privy Council of Scotland*, 3rd series, x (Edinburgh, 1927), 104–5.

80. Robert Chambers, *Domestic Annals of Scotland*, iii (Edinburgh, 1861), 290.

81. Ferguson, *op. cit.*, 85.

82. *Extracts from the Records of the Convention of the Royal Burghs of Scotland, 1677–1711* (Edinburgh, 1880), 577.

83. *Ibid.*, 578–9.

84. *Ibid.*, 591–2.

85. *Ibid.*, 593.

86. *Ibid.*, 594-5.

87. *Ibid.*, 610.

88. *Ibid.*, 620.

89. *Ibid.*, 626.

90. *Ibid.*, 629.

91. *Ibid.*, 641.

92. *Ibid.*, 570.

93. *Ibid.*, 576.

94. *Early Travellers in Scotland*, 256.

95. S. G. Checkland, *Scottish Banking: A History* (Glasgow and London, 1975), 26.

96. Ferguson, *op. cit.*, 82.

97. Checkland, *op. cit.*, 59.

98. Smout, *Scottish Trade on the Eve of Union*, 252. For a full account of the project and its collapse, *see* George Pratt Insh, *The Company of Scotland* (London and New York, 1932).

99. The subscription lists are published in *The Darien Papers* (Bannatyne Club, 1849), 371-417.

100. Chambers, *op. cit.*, iii, 302-3.

101. *Memoirs of the Life of Sir John Clerk of Penicuik*, ed. John M. Gray (Scottish History Society, 1892), 38.

102. [John Macky], *A Journey through Scotland* (London, 1723), 275-6.

103. Daniel Defoe, *A Tour Thro' the whole Island of Great Britain*, ed. G. D. H. Cole, ii (London, 1927), 733.

104. *Ibid.*, ii, 734.

105. Handley, *op. cit.*, 148-9.

106. *The Works of Adam Petrie* (Edinburgh, 1877), 11-12.

107. Smout, *Scottish Trade on the Eve of Union*, 10.

108. *Early Travellers in Scotland*, 278.

109. Handley, *op. cit.*, 30.

110. [Edmund Burt], *Burt's Letters from the North of Scotland*, i (Edinburgh, 1974), 79.

111. Chambers, *op. cit.*, iii, 86.

112. Ferguson, *op. cit.*, 193.

113. Ramsay, *op. cit.*, ii, 89.

114. *Ibid.*, ii, 90-1.

115. *Early Travellers in Scotland*, 265.

116. Ramsay, *op. cit.*, ii, 91n.

117. Fletcher, *op. cit.*, 141.

118. Defoe, *op. cit.*, ii, 834.

119. See the contract of 1704 between the Duke and Patrick Murray, printed in *Chronicles of the Atholl and Tullibardine Families*, ed. John, seventh Duke of Atholl, ii (Edinburgh, 1908), 45.

120. Sir William Fraser, *The Scotts of Buccleuch*, i (Edinburgh, 1878), 456.

121. W. C. Mackenzie, *The Life and Times of John Maitland, Duke of Lauderdale* (London and New York, 1923), 493.

122. Hugo Arnot, *The History of Edinburgh* (Edinburgh, 1779), 611-6.

123. Sir James Balfour Paul, *Heraldry in Relation to Scottish History and Art* (Edinburgh, 1900), 100-1.

124. *Ibid.*, 89-90.

125. Chambers, *op. cit.*, iii, 560-1.

126. J. H. Stevenson, *Heraldry in Scotland*, i (Glasgow, 1914), 94.

127. *Chronicles of the Atholl and Tullibardine Families*, ii, 369-70.

128. [Mackintosh], *op. cit.*, xix-xxi.

129. Bruce Lenman, *The Jacobite Risings in Britain, 1689-1746* (London, 1980), 278.

130. *Chronicles of the Atholl and Tullibardine Families*, ed. John, seventh Duke of Atholl, i (Edinburgh, 1908), 180.

131. Lenman, *op. cit.*, 278.

132. Andrew Lang, *A History of Scotland*, iv (Edinburgh and London, 1907), 521.

133. Alexander Murdoch, *'The People Above'* (Edinburgh, 1980), 2–21.

CHAPTER 2

1. *Early Travellers in Scotland*, ed. P. Hume Brown (Edinburgh, 1891), 260.

2. Alexander Fenton and Bruce Walker, *The Rural Architecture of Scotland* (Edinburgh, 1981), 51–6.

3. *Ibid.*, 73–83.

4. *Ibid.*, 100–1.

5. *Ibid.*, 59–68.

6. David Bremner, *The Industries of Scotland* (repr. Newton Abbot, 1969), 405–12.

7. *The Book of the Thanes of Cawdor* (Spalding Club, 1859), 391.

8. Ian G. Lindsay and Mary Cosh, *Inveraray and the Dukes of Argyll* (Edinburgh, 1973), 46.

9. National Library of Scotland, MS 14666, f.138.

10. Scottish Record Office, CS 230/A/2/1, 'Act and Commission William Lord Braco Against William Adams', 47, 73–4.

11. T. C. Smout, *Scottish Trade on the Eve of Union* (Edinburgh and London, 1963), 161.

12. N.L.S., MS 14429, f.54, John, fourth Marquess of Tweeddale to William Black, 11 May, 1730.

13. N.L.S., MS 14429, f.55, 'Accompt pd out anent My Lord Marquess of Tweeddales Stones', 4 June, 1730.

14. S.R.O., CS 230/A/2/1, 'Act and Commission William Lord Braco Against William Adams', 47.

15. Basil Skinner, *The Lime Industry in the Lothians* (Edinburgh, 1969), 10.

16. Alick Morrison, 'The Contullich Papers', *Transactions of the Gaelic Society of Inverness*, xliv (1964–6), 323, 335, 338.

17. N.L.S., MS 14653, ff.93–101, 147; N.L.S., MS 14651, ff.144–5, 147.

18. N.L.S., MS 16565, f.195, Sir Robert Dickson to Andrew Fletcher, Lord Milton, 1 October, 1736.

19. S.R.O., GD 248/196/3/38, unsigned letter to Sir Ludovick Grant of Grant, [1753].

20. William Fraser, *The Earls of Cromartie*, i (Edinburgh, 1876), 55.

21. *Chronicles of the Frasers*, ed. William Mackay (Scottish History Society, 1905), 414.

22. N.L.S., MS 14413, f.109, Charles, Lord Yester, to John, second Marquess of Tweeddale, 15 April, 1710.

23. N.L.S., MS 2911, f.26, Tour of Sir William Burrell, 1758.

24. Geoffrey Stell, 'Highland Garrisons, 1717–23: Bernera Barracks', *Post-Medieval Archaeology*, vii (1973), 22.

25. Daniel Defoe, *A Tour Thro' the whole Island of Great Britain*, ed. G.D.H. Cole, ii (London, 1927), 721.

26. N.L.S., MS 17692, f.28, 'Memorial relateing to the Additions to be made to the house of Roseneath', 7 August, 1745.

27. *Ibid.*, Mary Cosh, 'Building Problems at Inveraray', *Bulletin of the Scottish Georgian Society*, ii (1973), 63.

28. William Adam, *Vitruvius Scoticus*, ed. James Simpson (Edinburgh, 1980), 1.

29. Advertisement in *The Caledonian Mercury*, 12 May, 1743.

30. *Extracts from the Records of the Burgh of Edinburgh, 1665 to 1680*, ed. Marguerite Wood (Edinburgh and London, 1950), 316.

31. S.R.O., CH 2/1132/1, 133–5.

32. S.R.O., GD 150/2410.

33. *The Caledonian Mercury*, 1 May, 1732.

34. *Ibid.*, 10 March, 1743.

35. *Ibid.*, 12 May, 1743.

36. Bremner, *op. cit.*, 418.

37. N.L.S., MS 14637, f.142, obligation by William Hutchison, 2 January, 1663.

38. N.L.S., MS 14499, f.166, contract between John Niccoll and James Syme, 3 March, 1714.

39. *The Book of the Thanes of Cawdor*, 424.

40. Bremner, *op. cit.*, 424–6.

41. N.L.S., Acc. 7228, f.460, 'Articles of Agreement' between Patrick Stewart and William Rig, 8 August, 1719.

42. Advertisement in *Edinburgh Evening Courant*, 27 January, 1752.

43. T. C. Smout, 'Lead-mining in Scotland, 1650–1850', *Studies in Scottish Business History*, ed. Peter L. Payne (London, 1967), 104.

44. Smout, *Scottish Trade on the Eve of Union*, 10.

45. Smout, 'Lead-mining in Scotland, 1650–1850', 104–6.

46. N.L.S., MS 14666, f.136, 'Account of the Duke of Queensberry's lead Sent to Leith for my Lord Marquess of Tweeddales use', 1730.

47. N.L.S., MS 14411, f.55, Alexander Hay to John, second Earl of Tweeddale, 6 November, 1686.

48. John Shaw, *Water Power in Scotland, 1550–1870* (Edinburgh, 1984), 90.

49. *Ibid.*, 84–8.

50. Smout, *Scottish Trade on the Eve of Union*, 159–60.

51. N.L.S., MS 14551, f.24, contract between William Adam and John, fourth Marquess of Tweeddale, 20 December, 1729.

52. Defoe, *op. cit.*, ii, 698.

53. *Ibid.*, ii, 698.

54. Bruce Lenman, *The Jacobite Risings in Britain, 1689–1746* (London, 1980), 245–6.

55. Fraser, *op. cit.*, i, 55–6.

56. S.R.O., CS 230/A/2/1, 'Act and Commission William Lord Braco Against William Adams', 47.

57. Smout, *Scottish Trade on the Eve of Union*, 154 6.

58. N.L.S., MS 14623, f.251, receipt of Matthew McCallum, 3 December, 1686.

59. *The Book of the Thanes of Cawdor*, 424.

60. N.L.S., Acc. 7228, f.1.

61. Fraser, *op. cit.*, i, 56.

62. Smout, *Scottish Trade on the Eve of Union*, 163.

63. *Ibid.*, 180–2.

64. *Ibid.*, 156.

65. N.L.S., MS 16555, f.151, Colen Campbell to Andrew Fletcher, Lord Milton, 17 January, 1734.

66. N.L.S., MS 14429, f.150, John Park to John Leslie, 23 May, 1722.

67. N.L.S., MS 17692, f.28, 'Memorial relateing to the Additions to be made to the house of Roseneath', 7 August, 1745.

68. N.L.S., MS 17684, f.22, 'Memorial relating to the Work at the Castle of Inveraray', 29 September, 1746.

69. *The Register of the Privy Council of Scotland*, 3rd series, ix (Edinburgh, 1924), 250.

70. S.R.O., CS 230/A/2/1, 'State of the Process at the Instance of William Adams Architect against William Lord Braco', 3–4.

71. Cosh, *op. cit.*, 63.

72. [John Macky], *A Journal through Scotland* (London, 1723), 153.

73. Quoted in Cosh, *op. cit.*, 62.

74. S.R.O., GD 248/176/1/25, John Adam to Sir Ludovick Grant of Grant, 29 March, 1753.

75. S.R.O., CS 230/A/2/1, 'Act and Commission William Lord Braco Against William Adams', 117.

CHAPTER 3

1. J. Stewart Seggie and D. Lowe Turnbull, *Annals of the Lodge of Journeymen Masons No. 8* (Edinburgh, 1930), 28.

2. National Library of Scotland, MS 3577, Minute Book of the Culross Incorporation of Wrights, pp. 34–5.

3. *The Acts of the Parliaments of Scotland*, iii, (1804), 579.

4. In 1739 the Governors of Heriot's Hospital, Edinburgh, agreed that boys could be apprenticed under the age of sixteen. In 1747 the Governors of George Watson's Hospital, Edinburgh, decided to allow boys to be apprenticed to the Edinburgh Shipping Company but not under the age of fifteen. *See* Alexander Law, *Education in Edinburgh in the Eighteenth Century* (London, 1965), 132 and n. 133.

5. David Murray Lyon, *History of the Lodge of Edinburgh (Mary's Chapel), No. 1* (tercentenary edition [London], 1900), 32.

6. *The Records of the Trades House of Glasgow, A.D. 1605–1678* (Glasgow, 1910), 450, 453, 461–2, 483, 501–2, 516.

7. George Hay, *History of Arbroath* (Arbroath, 1876), 290.

8. N.L.S., MS 19240, Minute Book of the Incorporation of Hammermen of Perth, 5.

9. *Extracts from the Records of the Royal Burgh of Lanark* (Glasgow, 1893), 196.

10. N.L.S., MS 3577, Minute Book of the Culross Incorporation of Wrights, 25, 53.

11. *Ibid.*, 53; *Extracts from the Records of the Royal Burgh of Lanark*, 196.

12. N.L.S., MS 3577, Minute Book of the Culross Incorporation of Wrights, 25; N.L.S., Dep. 302/2, Minute Book of the United Incorporation of Mary's Chapel, 26.

13. City of Edinburgh District Council archives, Minute Book of the United Incorporation of Mary's Chapel, *passim*; *Register of Edinburgh Apprentices, 1666–1700*, ed. Charles Boog Watson (Scottish Record Society, lx, 1929), *passim*; *Register of Edinburgh Apprentices, 1701–1755*, ed. Charles Boog Watson (Scottish Record Society, lxi, 1929), *passim*.

14. N.L.S., MS 3577, Minute Book of the Culross Incorporation of Wrights, 48.

15. *Ibid.*, 58.

16. N.L.S., MS 19240, Minute Book of the Incorporation of Hammermen of Perth, 28.

17. N.L.S., MS 3577, Minute Book of the Culross Incorporation of Wrights, 71.

18. *Ibid.*, 85.

19. James Colston, *The Incorporated Trades of Edinburgh* (Edinburgh, 1891), 65. The Incorporation also included the coopers, bowyers and sievewrights.

20. City of Edinburgh District Council archives, Minute Book of the United Incorporation of Mary's Chapel, *passim*; N.L.S., Dep. 302/1, Minute Book of the United Incorporation of Mary's Chapel, *passim*.

21. City of Edinburgh District Council archives, Minute Book of the United Incorporation of Mary's Chapel, 30 April, 1709.

22. *Ibid.*, 25 September, 1686.

23. *Ibid.*, 28 September 1717.

24. *Ibid.*, 6 September, 1744.

25. *Ibid.*, 1 February, 1709.

26. *Ibid.*, 29 November, 1718.

27. *Ibid.*, 1 March, 1735.

28. *Ibid.*, 16 December, 1738.

29. *Ibid.*, 24 March, 1744.

30. *Ibid.*, 24 February, 1749.

31. *Ibid.*, 23 August, 1707.

32. *Ibid.*, 21 January, 1708.

33. *Ibid., passim.*

34. *Ibid.*, 26 March, 1692.

35. *Ibid., passim.*

36. *Ibid.*, 13 January, 1711.

37. *Ibid.*, 10 April, 1697.

38. *Ibid.*, 4 February, 1727.

39. *Ibid.*, 23 November, 1706.

40. *Ibid.*, 28 May, 1691.

41. *Ibid.*, 25 March, 1710.

42. *Ibid.*, 14 July, 1733.

43. N.L.S., Adv. MS 34.6.29, Account Book of William Baillie, 3–6.

44. N.L.S., MS 1109, f.221, James Smith to John Mackenzie of Delvine, 14 April, 1721.

45. S.R.O., CS 230/A/2/1, 'Act and Commission William Lord Braco Against William Adams, 52.

46. *Ibid.*, 137–8.

47. Quoted in Howard Colvin, *A Biographical Dictionary of British Architects, 1600–1840* (2nd edn, London, 1978), 59.

48. S.R.O., CS 230/A/2/1, 'Act and Commission William Lord Braco Against William Adams', 50.

CHAPTER 4

1. Alistair Rowan, 'George Heriot's Hospital, Edinburgh', *Country Life* (6 March, 1975), 555.

2. John Summerson, *Architecture in Britain, 1530–1830* (4th edn, 1963), 331.

3. Rowan, *op. cit.*, 556.

4. Quoted in John G. Dunbar, *The Historic Architecture of Scotland* (London, 1966), 68.

5. A. A. Tait, 'The Protectorate Citadels of Scotland', *Architectural History*, viii (1965), 12–14.

6. Robert Scott Mylne, *The Master Masons to the Crown of Scotland* (Edinburgh, 1893), 145.

7. M. E. Cumming Bruce, *Family Records of the Bruces and the Cumyns* (Edinburgh and London, 1870), 298.

8. John Dunbar, *Sir William Bruce* (Scottish Arts Council Exhibition Catalogue, Edinburgh, 1970), 1–2.

9. Howard Colvin, *A Biographical Dictionary of British Architects* (London, 1978), 151.

10. Robert Douglas, *The Baronage of Scotland* (Edinburgh, 1798), 245.

11. Colvin, *op. cit.*, 151–2 and n.

12. Joseph Foster, *Members of Parliament, Scotland* (2nd edn, London and Aylesbury, 1882), 41.

13. *The Acts of the Parliaments of Scotland*, viii (1820), 488.

14. Colvin, *op. cit.*, 152.

15. *Ibid.*, 152.

16. Douglas, *op. cit.*, 245

17. John Gifford, *The Buildings of Scotland: Fife* (Harmondsworth, 1988).

18. Daniel Defoe, *A Tour Thro' the whole Island of Great Britain*, ed. G. D. H. Cole, ii (London, 1927), 778.

19. Dunbar, *Sir William Bruce*, 10.

20. Colvin, *op. cit.*, 152.

21. The elevations and plans of Panmure are printed in William Adam, *Vitruvius Scoticus* [c.1812], pls. 129–31.

22. Gifford, *op. cit.*, 84–6.

23. John G. Dunbar, 'The Building-activities of the Duke and Duchess of Lauderdale', *The Archaeological Journal*, cxxxii (1975), 203–4.

24. *The Lauderdale Papers*, ed. Osmund Airy, ii (Camden Society, 1885), 188.

25. Colvin, *op. cit.*, 152.

26. Mylne, *op. cit.*, 164–75.

27. Colvin, *op. cit.*, 152.

28. Dunbar, 'The Building-activities of the Duke and Duchess of Lauderdale', 229–30.

29. Colvin, *op. cit.*, 154.

30. Alistair Rowan, 'The building of Hopetoun', *Architectural History*, xxvii (1984), 200n.

31. Plans of Coleshill are printed in [John] Woolfe and [James] Gandon, *Vitruvius Britannicus*, v ([London]), 1771, pl. 86, and of Kinross in Adam, *Vitruvius Scoticus*, pl. 61.

32. [John Macky], *A Journey through Scotland* (London, 1723), 171.

33. Colvin, *op. cit.*, 154.

34. Rowan, 'The building of Hopetoun', 183–5.

35. For which, see Colen Campbell, *Vitruvius Britannicus*, ii (London, 1717), pls. 35–6.

36. Rowan, 'The building of Hopetoun', 187.

37. See the plan in Campbell, *Vitruvius Britannicus*, ii, pl. 75.

38. *Ibid.*, ii, 4.

39. Quoted in Colvin, *op. cit.*, 153.

40. Scottish Record Office, GD 26/13/440, Sir William Bruce to George, first Earl of Melville, 2 April, 1697.

41. S.R.O., GD 26/13/272, Sir William Bruce to George, first Earl of Melville, 21 April, 1697.

42. Colvin, *op. cit.*, 282.

43. Campbell, *Vitruvius Britannicus*, ii, 3.

44. Colvin, *op. cit.*, 755.

45. National Library of Scotland, MS 1103, f.171, James Smith to John Mackenzie of Delvine, 11 March, 1714.

46. Colvin, *op. cit.*, 755.

47. City of Edinburgh District Council archives, Minute Book of the United Incorporation of Mary's Chapel, 10 April, 1680.

48. Colvin, *op. cit.*, 757.

49. *Records of Inverness*, ed. William Mackay and George Smith Laing, ii (New Spalding Club, 1924), 284.

50. Colvin, *op. cit.*, 755–6.

51. Adam, *Vitruvius Scoticus*, pl. 8.

52. *Ibid.*, pls. 23–4.

53. [Macky], *op. cit.*, 31–2.

54. Colvin, *op. cit.*, 756; H. M. Colvin, 'A Scottish origin for English Palladianism?', *Architectural History*, xvii (1974), 7.

55. S.R.O., GD 121/1/469, 'Ane Account of work done by Mr James Smith to My L[ord] Rosehaugh'.

56. S.R.O., GD 124/15/663/2, James Smith to John, eleventh Earl of Mar, 15 October, 1707.

57. e.g. S.R.O., GD 124/15/663/3, James Smith to John, eleventh Earl of Mar, 6 November, 1707; S.R.O., GD 124/15/471, James Smith to John, eleventh Earl of Mar, 6 November, 1707; S.R.O., GD 124/15/804/2, James Smith to John, eleventh Earl of Mar, 6 April, 1708.

58. S.R.O., GD 124/15/663/3, James Smith to John, eleventh Earl of Mar, 6 November, 1707.

59. Colvin, *A Biographical Dictionary of British Architects*, 296–7.

60. S.R.O., GD 124/15/449/56, John, eleventh Earl of Mar, to Sir David Nairne, 11 November, 1706.

61. Quoted in Colvin, *A Biographical Dictionary of British Architects*, 296.

62. [Macky], *op. cit.*, 181–2.

63. Colvin, *A Biographical Dictionary of British Architects*, 282–3.

64. Quoted in *Ibid.*, 283.

65. S.R.O., GD 124/15/219, Alexander Edward to John, eleventh Earl of Mar, 7 July, 1702.

66. S.R.O., GD 124/15/342, John, Marquess of Tullibardine, to John, eleventh Earl of Mar, 9 March, 1706.

67. S.R.O., GD 124/15/904/2, James, fourth Earl of Panmure, to John, eleventh Earl of Mar, 17 December, 1708.

68. S.R.O., GD 124/15/938, Alexander McGill to John, eleventh Earl of Mar, 18 December, 1708.

CHAPTER 5

1. Abbotshall Parish Baptismal Registers, ex. inf. William Kay.

2. Scottish Record Office, GD 18/4981, John Clerk of Eldin, 'Life of Robert Adam'.

3. Robert Douglas, *The Baronage of Scotland* (Edinburgh, 1798), 255–6.

4. *The Register of Marriages for the Parish of Edinburgh, 1595–1700*, ed. Henry Paton (Scottish Record Society, 1905), 3; information from William Kay.

5. James Turner, *Memoirs of his own Life and Times* (Bannatyne Club, 1829), 76, 79.

6. *The Scots Peerage*, ed. James Balfour Paul, ii (Edinburgh, 1905), 596.

7. John Nicoll, *A Diary of Public Transactions* (Bannatyne Club, 1836), 71.

8. *Scotland and the Protectorate*, ed. C. H. Firth (Scottish History Society, 1899), 44.

9. *The Scots Peerage*, ii, 596.

10. *Ibid.*, ii, 596.

11. *See The Register of the Privy Council of Scotland*, 3rd series, ii (Edinburgh, 1909), 99, 139–40.

12. *The Diary of Mr John Lamont of Newton* (Maitland Club, 1830), 140.

13. He was still living in 1673 but dead by 1678. *See The Register of the Privy Council of Scotland*, 3rd series, iv (Edinburgh, 1911), 9, and *Ibid.*, 3rd series, vi (Edinburgh, 1914), 53.

14. James T. Davidson, *The Linktown of Abbotshall*, ed. William Saunders (Kirkcaldy, 1951), 7.

15. George Brunton and David Haig, *An Historical Account of the Senators of the College of Justice* (Edinburgh, 1836), 399–401.

16. Quoted in Davidson, *op. cit.*, 25.

17. *The Acts of the Parliaments of Scotland*, viii (1820), 137–8.

18. Kirkcaldy Museum and Art Gallery, Act by Sir Andrew Ramsay, 30 May, 1678.

19. Kirkcaldy Museum and Art Gallery, Minute Book of the Incorporation of Hammermen of Linktown of Abbotshall, 20 February, 1702.

20. *Ibid.*, 4 August, 1710.

21. *The Acts of the Parliaments of Scotland*, viii, 139.

22. S.R.O., GD 26/6/152/3, 17–18.

23. Robert Sibbald, *The History of Fife and Kinross* (New edn, Cupar, 1803), 315.

24. L. Macbean, *The Kirkcaldy Burgh Records* (Kirkcaldy, 1908), 71–3.

25. *Ibid.*, 231.

26. John Campbell, *The Church and Parish of Kirkcaldy* (Kirkcaldy, 1904), 84–5.

27. Regulations of 28 August, 1705, quoted in *Ibid.*, 85.

28. *Ibid.*, 86–7.

29. Macbean, *op. cit.*, 229–30.

30. S.R.O., CS 230/A/2/1, 'Act and Commission William Lord Braco against William Adams', 139.

31. Kirkcaldy Museum and Art Gallery, Minute Book of the Incorporation of Hammermen of Linktown of Abbotshall, 9 May, 1704.

32. Perhaps about 1710. See William Adam, *Vitruvius Scoticus*, ed. James Simpson (Edinburgh, 1980), 1. But William Kay has found evidence that he may have lived about ten years longer.

33. Kirkcaldy Museum and Art Gallery, Minute Book of the Incorporation of Hammermen of Linktown of Abbotshall, *passim*.

34. Howard Colvin, *A Biographical Dictionary of British Architects* (London, 1978), 757.

35. S.R.O., GD 18/4736, William Adam to Sir John Clerk of Penicuik, 6 October, 1741.

36. S.R.O., GD 18/4981, John Clerk of Eldin, draft for a life of Robert Adam.

37. National Library of Scotland, MS 17263, f.94, 'Accompt of sclatter work wrough [*sic*.] be Thomas Murray to the laird of Salton at ye new miln', 5 November, 1711.

38. John Shaw, *Water Power in Scotland* (Edinburgh, 1984), 39.

39. James E. Handley, *Scottish Farming in the Eighteenth Century* (London, 1953), 217–8.

40. Articles of Agreement between Henry Fletcher and James Meikle, 17 April, 1710, printed in Robert Somerville, *General View of the Agriculture of East Lothian* (London, 1805), 294.

41. W. C. Mackenzie, *Andrew Fletcher of Saltoun* (Edinburgh, 1935), 303.

42. N.L.S., MS 17248, f.2, 'Articles of agreement betwixt Henry Fletcher for his brother the Laird of Salton, and James Meikle Master of the Work at the Barley-Milne at Salton', October, 1712.

43. Kirkcaldy Public Library, 'Linktown Potteries—Documents, 1714–1847', 2–3.

44. *Ibid.*, 4.

45. Adam, *Vitruvius Scoticus*, ed. Simpson, 1.

46. S.R.O., GD 150/2410.

47. Davidson, *op. cit.*, 89–91.

48. *The Register of the Privy Council of Scotland*, 3rd series, xv (Edinburgh, 1967), 473.

49. *The Darien Papers* (Bannatyne Club, 1849), 375.

50. Davidson, *op. cit.*, 80.

51. *Ibid.*, 92.

52. John Fleming, *Robert Adam and his Circle* (London, 1962), 323.

53. Davidson, *op. cit.*, 90.

54. Fleming, *op. cit.*, 323.

55. Adam, *Vitruvius Scoticus*, ed. Simpson, 1.

56. *Ibid.*, 1.

57. S.R.O., CII 2/154/6, 234.

CHAPTER 6

1. Scottish Record Office, CII 2/224/5, p. 287.

2. John Fleming, *Robert Adam and his Circle* (London, 1962), 45.

3. William Adam, *Vitruvius Scoticus*, ed. James Simpson (Edinburgh, 1980), 2.

4. A. A. Tait, *The Landscape Garden in Scotland, 1735–1835* (Edinburgh, 1980), 8, 35.

5. Adam, *Vitruvius Scoticus*, ed. Simpson, 2.

6. S.R.O., GD 158/2515, 119–20, copy, Alexander, second Earl of Marchmont, to William Adam, 12 September, 1724.

7. Howard Colvin, *A Biographical Dictionary of British Architects* (London, 1978), 57.

8. Annandale's principal house in Dumfriesshire, Lochwood Tower, had been burnt in 1710. William Fraser, *The Annandale Family Book*, i (Edinburgh 1894), cccxxxiv.

9. S.R.O., GD 18/4727, James, second Marquess of Annandale, to Sir John Clerk of Penicuik, 23 January, 1724.

10. Geoffrey Stell, 'Highland Garrisons, 1717–23: Bernera Barracks', *Post-Medieval Archaeology*, vii (1973), 21–2.

11. S.R.O., GD 18/5004, James Smith to Sir John Clerk of Penicuik, 12 December, 1720.

12. Colvin, *op. cit.*, 758. It is possible that House of Gray which was being built in 1723 is also by Smith and McGill.

13. *Ibid.*, 571.

14. *Ibid.*, 756.

15. S.R.O., GD 18/4982, John Clerk of Eldin draft for a life of Robert Adam.

16. *Catalogue: Blair-Adam Library, 1883* (London, 1883), *passim*.

17. S.R.O., GD 18/4729/2, William Adam to Sir John Clerk of Penicuik, 5 May, 1726.

18. Colen Campbell, *Vitruvius Britannicus*, i (London, 1715), 9–10; *Ibid.*, ii (London, 1717), 7–8.

19. S.R.O., GD 158/2507, pp. 266–7, Alexander, Lord Polwarth, to Sir James Hall of Dunglass, 8 January, 1724.

20. S.R.O., GD 158/2507, 269; Alexander, Lord Polwarth, to Sir James Hall of Dunglass, 8 January 1724.

21. S.R.O., GD 158/2515, copy, Alexander, second Earl of Marchmont, to Sir James Hall of Dunglass, 15 December, 1724.

22. S.R.O., GD 18/4982, John Clerk of Eldin, draft for a life of Robert Adam.

23. S.R.O., GD 18/4728/3, William Adam to Sir John Clerk of Penicuik, 20 October, 1724.

24. *Memoirs of the Life, Family, and Character of John late Earl of Stair* (London, [1747]), 39.

25. John Murray Graham, *Annals and Correspondence of the Viscount and the first and second Earls of Stair*, ii (Edinburgh, 1875), 161–2.

26. J. H. Plumb, *Sir Robert Walpole*, ii (London, 1960), 105.

27. Alistair Rowan, 'The building of Hopetoun', *Architectural History*, xxvii (1984), 191.

28. David and Francina Urwin, *Scottish Painters at Home and Abroad, 1700–1900* (London, 1975), 100.

29. Quoted in Iain Gordon Brown, 'Sir John Clerk of Penicuik (1676–1755): Aspects of a Virtuoso Life', unpublished Ph.D. thesis, Cambridge University, 1980, 15.

30. Quoted in *Ibid.*, 59.

31. Colvin, *op. cit.*, 219.

32. Fleming, *op. cit.*, 17.

33. Brown, *op. cit.*, 78.

34. *Memoirs of the Life of Sir John Clerk of Penicuik*, ed. John M. Gray (Scottish History Society, xiii, 1892), 34.

35. Colvin, *op. cit.*, 219.

36. Brown, *op. cit.*, 167.

37. *Memoirs of the Life of Sir John Clerk of Penicuik*, 232.

38. *Ibid., passim.*

39. Fleming, *op. cit.*, 20–1.

40. Brown, *op. cit.*, 91.

41. Colvin, *op. cit.*, 219.

42. Quoted in Brown, *op. cit.*, 257.

43. *Ibid.*, 257.

44. Quoted in Fleming, *op. cit.*, 26.

45. Brown, *op. cit.*, 235.

46. *Ibid.*, 262.

47. *Memoirs of the Life of Sir John Clerk of Penicuik*, 149.

48. Quoted in Brown, *op. cit.*, 261.

49. Stuart Piggott, 'Sir John Clerk and The Country Seat', *The Country Seat*, ed. Howard Colvin and John Harris (London, 1970), 112.

50. [George Lockhart], *Memoirs Concerning the Affairs of Scotland* (London, 1714), 107.

51. Richard Pococke, *Tours in Scotland*, ed. Daniel William Kemp (Scottish History Society, i, 1887), 330.

52. Colen Campbell, *Vitruvius Britannicus*, iii (London, 1725), 8 and pl. 40.

53. The decision to rebuild Houghton seems to have been taken in the summer of 1720 and designs were presumably produced at that time. Howard E. Stutchbury, *The Architecture of Colen Campbell* (Manchester, 1967), 149.

54. Daniel Defoe, *A Tour Thro' the whole Island of Great Britain*, ed. G. D. H. Cole, ii (London, 1927), 764–5.

55. As pointed out in Rowan, *op. cit.*, 189.

56. *The Scots Peerage*, ed. James Balfour Paul, iv (Edinburgh, 1907), 494–7.

57. Campbell, *Vitruvius Britannicus*, i, pl. 42.

58. [John Macky], *A Journey through Scotland* (London, 1723), 205–6.

59. Rowan, *op. cit.*, 190–1.

60. *Ibid.*, 192–3.

61. Tait, *op. cit.*, 27.

62. [Macky], *op. cit.*, 206–7.

63. *Memoirs of the Life of Sir John Clerk of Penicuik*, 113–4.

64. S.R.O., GD 18/4719, William Adam to Sir John Clerk of Penicuik, 30 January, 1723.

65. *Ibid.* In Fleming, *op. cit.*, 34, it is suggested that Adam had proposed an attic between the main cornice and the eaves of the type produced by Bruce at Kinross House.

66. *Memoirs of the Life of Sir John Clerk of Penicuik*, 115.

67. S.R.O., GD 18/4719, William Adam to Sir John Clerk of Penicuik, 30 January, 1723.

68. *Memoirs of the Life of Sir John Clerk of Penicuik*, 114–5.

69. *Ibid.*, 115.

70. S.R.O., GD 18/4719, William Adam to Sir John Clerk of Penicuik, 30 January, 1723.

71. Brown, *op. cit.*, 184.

72. Quoted in Piggott, *op. cit.*, 115.

73. *Ibid.*, 114.

74. *Ibid.*, 114.

75. S.R.O., GD 18/4726, William Adam to Sir John Clerk of Penicuik, 21 August, 1723.

76. S.R.O., GD 18/4728/3, William Adam to Sir John Clerk of Penicuik, 20 October, 1724.

77. S.R.O., GD 18/4735/2, William Adam to Sir John Clerk of Penicuik, 4 May, 1725.

78. *Ibid.*

79. S.R.O., GD 18/4728/12, William Adam to Sir John Clerk of Penicuik, 16 April, 1725.

80. Tait, *op. cit.*, 21–3.

81. *Memoirs of the Life of Sir John Clerk of Penicuik*, 132.

82. S.R.O., GD 18/4729/5, William Adam to Sir John Clerk of Penicuik, 20 December, 1727.

83. Geoffrey Beard, *Decorative Plasterwork in Great Britain* (London, 1975), 83–4.

84. S.R.O., GD 18/4728/10, William Adam to Sir John Clerk of Penicuik, 15 May, 172[8].

85. Joseph Foster, *Members of Parliament, Scotland* (2nd edn, London and Aylesbury, 1882), 135.

86. The engraving in *Vitruvius Scoticus* shows the house with a segmental pediment. The pediment is now triangular.

87. *The Scots Peerage*, ed. James Balfour Paul, viii (Edinburgh, 1911), 33–6.

88. S.R.O., GD 18/4729/2, William Adam to Sir John Clerk of Penicuik, 5 May, 1726.

89. Colvin, *op. cit.*, 57.

90. *The Scots Peerage*, viii, 154.

91. Colvin, *op. cit.*, 57.

92. *Ibid.*, 57.

93. John Ramsay of Ochtertyre, *Scotland and Scotsmen in the Eighteenth Century*, ed. Alexander Allardyce, i (Edinburgh, 1888), 71–2.

94. George W. T. Omond, *The Lord Advocates of Scotland*, i (Edinburgh, 1883), 311–4.

95. The fullest published account of Arniston's building history is given in Mary Cosh, 'The Adam family and Arniston', *Architectural History*, xxvii (1984), 214–23.

96. Tait, *op. cit.*, 27–8.

97. S.R.O., GD 18/4722, William Adam to Sir John Clerk of Penicuik, 28 March, 1723.

98. S.R.O., GD 18/4723, Charles, first Earl of Hopetoun, to Sir John Clerk of Penicuik, 6 April, 1723.

99. *An Act for Enlarging the Term granted in the Third Year of His Majesty's Reign (for Continuing the Duty of Two Pennies Scots upon every Pint of Ale and Beer sold in the City of Edinburgh . . .) and for making the said Act more effectual* (London, 1723), 481.

100. *Ibid.*, 490.

101. Colvin, *op. cit.*, 56. It was probably to some confused family story about this episode that John Clerk of Eldin referred when he wrote that the conferring of a baronetcy on William Adam had been prevented by George I's death. S.R.O., GD 18/4982, John Clerk of Eldin, draft for a life of Robert Adam.

102. S.R.O., GD 18/4730, Sir John Anstruther of Anstruther to Sir John Clerk of Penicuik, 20 December, 1727.

103. Colvin, *op. cit.*, 56.

104. S.R.O., GD 18/4729/2, William Adam to Sir John Clerk of Penicuik, 5 May, 1726.

105. Fleming, *op. cit.*, 22-3; *Memoirs of the Life of Sir John Clerk of Penicuik*, 121-3.

106. *Memoirs of the Life of Sir John Clerk of Penicuik*, 130.

107. *Ibid.*, 124-9.

108. Fleming, *op. cit.*, 7; Duncan Macmillan, *Painting in Scotland: the Golden Age* (Oxford, 1986), 14.

109. S.R.O., GD 18/4729/5, William Adam to Sir John Clerk of Penicuik, 20 December, 1727.

110. Quoted in Colvin, *op. cit.*, 56n.

111. There were probably no more than 150 subscribers for *Vitruvius Scoticus*. By contrast there were about 700 for the third volume of Colen Campbell's *Vitruvius Britannicus* published in 1725 and 481 for James Gibbs' *A Book of Architecture* of 1728.

112. Adam, *Vitruvius Scoticus*, ed. Simpson, 7.

113. Quoted in Fleming, *op. cit.*, 7.

114. *Roll of Edinburgh Burgesses and Guild-Brethren, 1701-1760*, ed. Charles B. Boog Watson (Scottish Record Society, 1930), 1.

115. Colvin, *op. cit.*, 56.

116. *Ibid.*, 45-6; Robert Douglas, *The Baronage of Scotland* (Edinburgh, 1798), 256.

117. James T. Davidson, *The Linktown of Abbotshall*, ed. William Saunders (Kirkcaldy, 1951), 91.

CHAPTER 7

1. Scottish Record Office, CS 230/A/2/1, 'Act and Commission William Lord Braco Against William Adams', 113.

2. Replaced in 1822.

3. John Fleming, *Robert Adam and his Circle* (London, 1962), 9-13.

4. S.R.O., GD 18/5005/1, William, second Earl of Aberdeen, to Sir John Clerk of Penicuik, 5 December, 1731.

5. Howard Colvin, *A Biographical Dictionary of British Architects* (London, 1978), 220.

6. S.R.O., GD 18/5005/1, William, second Earl of Aberdeen, to Sir John Clerk of Penicuik, 5 December, 1731.

7. S.R.O., GD 18/5005/2, John Baxter to Sir John Clerk of Penicuik, 14 September, 1732.

8. S.R.O., GD 18/5005/3, John Baxter to Sir John Clerk of Penicuik, 2 July, 1733.

9. National Library of Scotland, MS 5074, f.148, Sir John Clerk of Penicuik to Charles Erskine of Tinwald, 5 April, 1739.

10. N.L.S., MS 5074, f.163, John, Lord Hope, to Charles Erskine of Tinwald, 11 April, 1739.

11. N.L.S., MS 5074, f.167, John, Lord Hope, to Charles Erskine of Tinwald, 13 April, 1739.

12. The fullest account of the development of Hopetoun is given in Alistair Rowan, 'The building of Hopetoun', *Architectural History*, xxvii (1984).

13. George Brunton and David Haig, *An Historical Account of the Senators of the College of Justice* (Edinburgh, 1836), 491.

14. James Ramsay of Ochtertyre, *Scotland and Scotsmen in the Eighteenth Century*, ed. Alexander Allardyce (Edinburgh, 1888), 84-6.

15. S.R.O., GD 123/120, 'Explanation of the new Design of a House Gardens & Parks for L^d. D-'.

16. *Ibid.*

17. *Ibid.*

18. *Ibid.*; S.R.O., RHP 13288.

19. Margaret C. H. Stewart, 'An Exiled Jacobite's Architectural Activities: Lord Mar's "House J", its Variants and related Projects (1716-1731)', *The Architectural Heritage Society of Scotland Journal and Annual Report*, xiv (1987), 17.

20. William Adam, *Vitruvius Scoticus* (n.p., c. 1812), pls. 69-70.

21. *Ibid.*, pl. 70.

22. James Gibbs, *A Book of Architecture* (London, 1728), pl. 37.

23. Stewart, *op. cit.*, 23.

24. Information from William Kay; Geoffrey Beard, *Decorative Plasterwork in Great Britain* (London, 1975), 84.

25. S.R.O., GD 18/4728/9, William Adam to Sir John Clerk of Penicuik, n.d.

26. S.R.O., GD 18/4729/1, William Adam to Sir John Clerk of Penicuik, 8 March, 1726.

27. N.L.S., MS 14660, f.80, 'Accot^t of Incidents from the 1st June to the 8 Octb^r 1726'.

28. N.L.S., MS 14420, f.1, Susan, Marchioness of Tweeddale, to John, 4th Marquess of Tweeddale, 15 April, 1716.

29. N.L.S., MS 14551, f.30, William Adam to John, 4th Marquess of Tweeddale, [1729].

30. *Ibid.*

31. S.R.O., GD 18/4731, John, fourth Marquess of Tweeddale, to Sir John Clerk of Penicuik, 21 October, 1729.

32. N.L.S., MS 14551, f.22, contract between John, fourth Marquess of Tweeddale, and William Adam, 20 December, 1729.

33. N.L.S., MS 14551, f.24, continuation of contract between John, fourth Marquess of Tweeddale, and William Adam, 20 December, 1729.

34. N.L.S., MS 14551, f.34, William Adam to

John, fourth Marquess of Tweeddale, 25 April, 1730.

35. N.L.S., MS 14551, f.36, William Adam to John, fourth Marquess of Tweeddale, 4 November, 1731.

36. N.L.S., MS 14551, f.41, William Adam, 'Memorandum relating to some work to be done att Yester', 18 October, 1734.

37. *Ibid.*

38. N.L.S., MS 14551, f.59.

39. N.L.S., MS 14552, f.186, 'Inventory The Furniture of Yester House', 20 April, 1737.

40. N.L.S., MS 14666, f.1, account book of Joseph Enzer, 1736-9.

41. N.L.S., MS 14668, f.43, account of Joseph Enzer, 23 February, 1740.

42. N.L.S., MS 14551, f.93, William Adam to John, fourth Marquess of Tweeddale, 5 July, 1743.

43. N.L.S., MS 14551, f.70, John, fourth Marquess of Tweeddale, to William Adam, 17 March, 1743.

44. N.L.S., MS 14551, f.77, William Adam to John, fourth Marquess of Tweeddale, 9 April, 1743.

45. N.L.S., MS 14551, f.72, 'Memorial relating to the Front Stair of Yester'.

46. *Ibid.*

47. N.L.S., MS 14551, f.87, John, fourth Marquess of Tweeddale, to William Adam, 28 April, 1743.

48. N.L.S., MS 14425, f.159, Thomas Hay to John, fourth Marquess of Tweeddale, 11 August, 1744.

49. N.L.S., MS 14551, f.103, William Adam to John, fourth Marquess of Tweeddale, 18 July, 1745.

50. *Ibid.*

51. *Ibid.*

52. N.L.S., MS 14551, f.51, William Adam, 'Memorandum relating to some work to be done att Yester', 18 October, 1734.

53. N.L.S., MS 14551, f.103, William Adam to John, fourth Marquess of Tweeddale, 18 July, 1745.

54. *Ibid.*

55. *The Scots Peerage*, ed. James Balfour Paul, iv (Edinburgh, 1907), 392.

56. S.R.O., GD 31/554, 'Report on the Claim John Adams Architect . . . against the Duke of Hamilton, 1770'.

57. Colvin, *op. cit.*, 758.

58. [John Macky], *A Journey through Scotland* (London, 1723), 283.

59. Gibbs, *op. cit.*, pl. 49.

60. [Macky], *op. cit.*, 282-3.

61. *The Scots Peerage*, iv, 367.

62. A. A. Tait, 'William Adam at Chatelherault', *The Burlington Magazine* (June, 1968), 319.

63. Quoted in *Ibid.*, 319-20.

64. *Ibid.*, 325n.

65. Quoted in Beard, *op. cit.*, 85.

66. Tait, *op. cit.*, 324n.

67. Beard, *op. cit.*, 85.

68. Quoted in Fleming, *op. cit.*, 59.

69. *Ibid.*, 59.

70. *Ibid.*, 60.

71. Robert Douglas, *The Peerage of Scotland* (2nd edn., revised by John Philip Wood, Edinburgh, 1813), 577.

72. Fleming, *op. cit.*, 52.

73. Quoted in Alistair and Henrietta Tayler, *The Book of the Duffs*, i (Edinburgh, 1914), 108.

74. Douglas, *op. cit.*, 577.

75. S.R.O., CS 230/A/2/1, 'Act and Commission William Lord Braco Against William Adams', 1.

76. *Ibid.*, 45.

77. *Ibid.*, 45–6.

78. *Ibid.*, 76.

79. *Ibid.*, 76.

80. *Ibid.*, 77.

81. *Ibid.*, 78.

82. *Ibid.*, 76.

83. James Simpson, 'The Building of Duff House', *Transactions of the Royal Archaeological Institute*, cxxx (1973), 221.

84. S.R.O., CS 230/A/2/1, 'Act and Commission William Lord Braco Against William Adams', 79.

85. *Ibid.*, 81.

86. Quoted in Tayler, *op. cit.*, i, 110.

87. N.L.S., MS 16555, f.8, William Adam to Andrew Fletcher, Lord Milton, 22 March, 1734.

88. John Gifford, Colin McWilliam and David Walker, *The Buildings of Scotland: Edinburgh* (Harmondsworth, 1984), 558–9.

89. N.L.S., MS 16564, f.4, William Adam to Andrew Fletcher, Lord Milton, 15 May, 1736.

90. N.L.S., MS 16564, f.5, William Adam to Andrew Fletcher, Lord Milton, 11 August, 1736.

91. N.L.S., MS 16575, f.134, William Smith to Andrew Fletcher, Lord Milton, 30 December, 1738.

92. Colvin, *op. cit.*, 58.

93. N.L.S., MS 16583, f.259, copy, Andrew Fletcher, Lord Milton, to [William Smith], 1740.

94. Alexander Murdoch, *'The People Above'* (Edinburgh, 1980), 6–8.

95. The Royal Commission on the Ancient and Historical Monuments of Scotland, *Peeblesshire*, ii (Edinburgh, 1967), 326.

96. Quoted in *Ibid.*, ii, 327.

97. N.L.S., MS 16542, f.47, Archibald, Earl of Ilay, to Andrew Fletcher, Lord Milton, 23 May, 1730.

98. N.L.S., MS 16542, f.1, William Adam to Andrew Fletcher, Lord Milton, 28 August, 1730.

99. N.L.S., MS 16548, f.5, William Adam to Andrew Fletcher, Lord Milton, 20 May, 1732.

100. The Royal Commission on the Ancient and Historical Monuments of Scotland, *op. cit.*, ii, 327.

101. N.L.S., MS 17643, f.9, memorandum about The Whim, 1733.

102. Colvin, *op. cit.*, 101–2.

103. N.L.S., MS 16596, f.4, William Adam to Andrew Fletcher, Lord Milton, 23 August, 1744.

104. Ian G. Lindsay and Mary Cosh, *Inveraray and the Dukes of Argyll* (Edinburgh, 1973), 46.

105. Quoted in Fleming, *op. cit.*, 65.

106. *Ibid.*, 65.

107. Mary Cosh, 'Building Problems at Inveraray', *Bulletin of the Scottish Georgian Society*, ii (1973), 62.

CHAPTER 8

1. Howard Colvin, *A Biographical Dictionary of British Architects* (London, 1978), 57.

2. Robert Anderson, *The History of Robert Gordon's Hospital, Aberdeen* (Aberdeen, 1896), 2-4.

3. *Ibid.*, 14-16.

4. *Ibid.*, 27-8.

5. Quoted in *Ibid.*, 28.

6. *Ibid.*, 34.

7. C. H. Collins Baker and Muriel I. Baker, *The Life and Circumstances of James Brydges, first Duke of Chandos* (Oxford, 1949), 101-2; James Coutts, *A History of the University of Glasgow* (Glasgow, 1909), 253.

8. Coutts, *op. cit.*, 253.

9. Colvin, *op. cit.*, 57.

10. Coutts, *op. cit.*, 254.

11. *An Historical Account of the Orphan Hospital of Edinburgh* (Edinburgh, 1833), 5-6.

12. *A Further Account of the State of the Orphan-School, Hospital and Workhouse at Edinburgh* (Edinburgh, 1736), 8.

13. *Ibid.*, 4.

14. *A Brief Account of the Rise, Progress, Management and State of the Orphan-School, Hospital and Work-house at Edinburgh* (Edinburgh, 1735), 6.

15. Alexander Heron, *The Rise and Progress of the Company of Merchants of the City of Edinburgh, 1681-1902* (Edinburgh, 1903), 83-6.

16. *Ibid.*, 84.

17. Edinburgh Central Public Library, typescript, 'Memorial for the Committee of the GOVERNORS OF GEORGE WATSON'S HOSPITAL to the TRUSTEES of the said George Watson', 3.

18. William Cowan, 'The Site of the Black Friars'

Monastery from the Reformation to the Present Day', *The Book of the Old Edinburgh Club*, v (1912), 81.

19. National Library of Scotland, MS 17871, f.17, 'Estimate of Mr George Watson's Hospital', 21 April, 1738.

20. Cowan, *op. cit.*, 79-80.

21. Quoted in Cowan, *op. cit.*, 82.

22. A. Logan Turner, *Story of a Great Hospital* (Edinburgh and London, 1937), 85.

23. Quoted in Robert Thin, 'The Old Infirmary and Earlier Hospitals', *The Book of the Old Edinburgh Club*, xv (1927), 153.

24. Turner, *op. cit.*, 90.

25. *A Letter from a Gentleman in Town to his Friend in the Country Relating to the Royal Infirmary of Edinburgh* (Edinburgh, 1739), 7-8.

26. *Ibid.*, 8.

27. *Ibid.*, 9.

28. *The History and Statutes of the Royal Infirmary of Edinburgh* (Edinburgh, 1749), 7.

29. *Ibid.*, 7.

30. Scottish Record Office, GD 18/4732/1, William Adam to Sir John Clerk of Penicuik, 11 February, 1729.

31. W. Forbes Gray, 'Gleanings from Scottish Exchequer Reports', *The Book of the Old Edinburgh Club*, xxiii (1940), 41.

32. John Fleming, *Robert Adam and his Circle* (London, 1962), 333.

33. *Ibid.*, 64.

34. N.L.S., MS 10693, pp. 222-6.

35. Fleming, *op. cit.*, 336.

36. N.L.S., MS 16559, f.11, William Adam to Andrew Fletcher, Lord Milton, 9 October, 1735. Captain John Lambertus Romer was in charge of the adminstration of the ordnance districts of Scotland and the north of England.

CHAPTER 9

1. National Library of Scotland, Acc. 7344/1, William Adam to Joseph Wardrop, 24 January, 1733.

2. N.L.S., Acc. 7344/1, Minutes of the Incorporation of Mary's Chapel, 22 and 24 December, 1733.

3. N.L.S., Acc. 7344/1, William Adam to Joseph Wardrop, 9 December, 1735.

4. *Ibid.*

5. *The Caledonian Mercury,* 18 February, 1745.

6. Howard Colvin, *A Biographical Dictionary of British Architects* (London, 1978), 58.

7. Edinburgh Central Public Library, Boog Watson Notes, ix, 155.

8. John Fleming, *Robert Adam and his Circle* (London, 1962), 333.

9. *Ibid.,* 333.

10. William Adam, *Vitruvius Scoticus,* ed. James Simpson (Edinburgh, 1980), 3.

11. Fleming, *op. cit.,* 52.

12. [William Adam], *The Progress of an Estate in Scotland* ([Blair Adam], c. 1835), 7.

13. Fleming, *op. cit.,* 52.

14. *Edinburgh Evening Courant,* 2 May, 1764.

15. [Adam], *The Progess of an Estate,* 7–8.

16. *Ibid.,* 11.

17. *Ibid.,* 8.

18. *Ibid.,* 8.

19. *Ibid.,* 11.

20. Adam, *Vitruvius Scoticus,* ed. Simpson, 3.

21. Scottish Record Office, GD 18/4982, John Clerk of Eldin, draft life of Robert Adam.

22. S.R.O., GD 31/554, 'Report on the Claim John Adams . . . against the Duke of Hamilton, 1770'.

23. *Edinburgh Evening Courant,* 24 August, 1736.

24. N.L.S., MS 16564, f.5, William Adam to Andrew Fletcher, Lord Milton, 11 August, 1736.

25. Fleming, *op. cit.,* 52.

26. William Maitland, *The History of Edinburgh* (Edinburgh, 1753), 504–5.

27. N.L.S., MS 14425, f.338, Thomas Hay to John, fourth Marquess of Tweeddale, 29 December, 1744.

28. S.R.O., CS 230/A/2/1, 'Act and Commission William Lord Braco Against William Adams', 117.

29. David and Francina Urwin, *Scottish Painters at Home and Abroad, 1700–1900* (London, 1975), 83.

30. Adam, *Vitruvius Scoticus,* ed. Simpson, 7.

31. Photograph in the National Monuments Record of Scotland.

32. Adam, *Vitruvius Scoticus,* ed. Simpson, 7.

33. James Simpson, 'The Building of Duff House', *Transactions of the Royal Archaeological Institute,* cxxx (1973), 221–2.

34. Quoted in Alistair and Henrietta Tayler, *The Book of the Duffs,* i (Edinburgh, 1914), 109.

35. *Ibid.,* i, 110.

36. *Ibid.,* i, 112.

37. Quoted in *Ibid.,* i, 115.

38. Quoted in Fleming, *op. cit.,* 54.

39. N.L.S., MS 16580, f.3, William Adam to Andrew Fletcher, Lord Milton, 13 March, 1740.

40. Quoted in Fleming, *op. cit.,* 54.

41. N.L.S., MS 16640, f.29, William Adam to Andrew Fletcher, Lord Milton, 15 December, 1747.

42. *Ibid.*

43. N.L.S., MS 16640, f.31, William Adam to Andrew Fletcher, Lord Milton, 19 December, 1747.

44. N.L.S., MS 16655, f.17, William Adam to Andrew Fletcher, Lord Milton, 29 January, 1748.

45. Adam, *Vitruvius Scoticus*, ed. Simpson, 4; Colvin, *op. cit.*, 44, 56.

46. Fleming, *op. cit.*, 76–81.

47. N.L.S., MS 16613, f.46, William Adam to Andrew Fletcher, Lord Milton, 26 September, 1746.

48. S.R.O., GD 18/4981, [John Clerk of Eldin], 'Life of Robert Adam'.

49. Quoted in Fleming, *op. cit.*, 336.

50. *The Caledonian Mercury*, 30 June, 1748.

List of Illustrations

Index

Lonmay House, 112, 114; *115*
Lorini, Buonanito, 51
Lothian, William, third Earl of, 49
Lothians, 13, 35
Low Countries, 72
Lyon King of Arms, Lord, 26

Maastricht, Town Hall, 61
McCallum, Matthew, 36
McDowall, John, 111
McGill, Alexander, 67, 77, 128, 129
Mackenzie, John (of Delvine), 46, 62
Mackintosh, William (of Borlum), 14, 15, 27
Macky, John, 23, 63, 66, 88, 89, 144, 146
Mar, John, eleventh Earl of, 66, 67, 128-9, 131; *65*
Marchmont, Alexander, second Earl of, 76, 79, 99, 111; *78*
Mark, John, 43
Marly, Château de, 61, 99
Marot, Jean, 78
Maryburgh, 178
Maurat, Carolo, 67
Mavisbank House, 9, 76, 90-5, 96, 98, 104, 108, 112, 121, 133; *91*
May, Hugh, 57
Medina, Sir John, 156, 158
Megginch, 32
Meikle, James, 73
Mellerstain, 76, 99, 104; *98*
Melville, George, first Earl of, 62
Melville, Walter, 43
Melville House, 60; *59*
Methil, 16
Millar, James, 43
Miller, William, 94
Milton, Andrew Fletcher, Lord, 28-9, 31, 36, 112, 155-6, 158, 159, 160, 174, 178, 180-2, 183; *155*
Milton House, 145
Minto, Sir Gilbert Elliot, Lord, 112, 176
Mitchell, Thomas, 20
Moncreiffe House, 57
Moncrieff, James, 41
Monk, General George, 51, 52
Montrose, 68
Montrose, James, third Marquess of, 53
Montrose, James, first Duke of, 108, 112, 165
Moray Firth, 15
Morayshire, 31
Mordaunt, Lady Henrietta: see Gordon, Henrietta, Duchess of
Morer, Thomas, 16, 17, 24
Morrice, Walter, 88
Morris, Roger, 140, 161, 162
Mount Stuart, 112, 117
Mowbray, Mr., 183
Munro, Sir Robert (of Foulis), 26
Murray, Mr., 107

Musselburgh, 36
Mylne, John, 51, 53, 54, 113, 156
Mylne, Robert (1633-1710), 53, 55, 57, 62, 63, 77
Mylne, Robert (1733-1811), 62

Nails, 34, 37
National Land Fund, 9
Newhailes, 33, 36, 77
Newhall, 8
Newliston House, 76, 81, 90, 99, 104; *100*
Nichols, Francis, 138
Niddrie Marischal, 111
Norie, James, 43, 148
Norie Family, 179
Norrköping, 31
Norway, 35, 36
Norwood, Robert, 51

Ormiston, 24
Ostend, 72
Oxford, Edward, second Earl of, 108
Oxford, The Queen's College, 147

Pains, William, 40
Palladio, Andrea, 44, 64, 65, 66, 78, 98
Panama, 23
Panmure, James, fourth Earl of, 67
Panmure House, 54; *54*
Pantiles, 32-3, 73-5
Paper mill, 19
Papillon, David, 51
Paris, 79, 81
    Hôtel Tambonneau, 61
    University, 127
Parliament of Great Britain, 28
Parliament of Scotland, 28
Paterson, James, 44
Peeblesshire, 33
Pembroke, Henry, ninth Earl of, 140
Pembroke, Thomas, eight Earl of, 108
Penicuik House, 90
Perth, 21, 22, 40, 41, 42; *19*
    Citadel, 51
Petrie, Adam, 24
Pinkie, 36, 178
Pitkennie, Laird of, younger, 75
Pittenweem, 22
Poland, 69
Polwarth, Alexander, Lord: see Marchmont, Alexander, second Earl of
Porcelain factories, 19
Porrelle, 43
Port Seton, 16, 31
Post, Pieter, 61
Pratt, Sir Roger, 57, 58
Preston, Sir Robert (of Valleyfield), 51
Prestonhall, 112, 115; *116*
Privy Council of Scotland, 21, 24, 28
Pumping, 17, 30